THE GOD WHO PROVIDES

THE GOD WHO PROVIDES

BIBLICAL IMAGES OF DIVINE NOURISHMENT

L. JULIANA M. CLAASSENS

Abingdon Press
Nashville

THE GOD WHO PROVIDES
BIBLICAL IMAGES OF DIVINE NOURISHMENT

Library of Congress Cataloging-in-Publication Data

Claassens, L. Juliana M., 1972-
    The God who provides : biblical images of divine nourishment / L. Juliana M. Claassens.
        p. cm.
    Includes bibliographical references and index.
    ISBN 0-687-03023-4 (bdg. : pbk. : alk. paper)
    1. Femininity of God—Biblical teaching.   2. Food in the Bible.   I. Title.
    BS544.C58 2004
    231—dc22

                                                                    2004002412

04 05 06 07 08 09 10 11 12 13—10 9 8 7 6 5 4 3 2 1

MANUFACTURED IN THE UNITED STATES OF AMERICA

To Donald H. Juel (1942–2003),
who created the space for this book
to come into being

CONTENTS

ACKNOWLEDGMENTS

As in any project of this nature, *The God Who Provides* has had a long and interesting journey from the first idea to the final product. Such a process includes many people and voices, so allow me to express my sincere thanks to the following people.

The God Who Provides had its very first beginnings in the New Testament theology class of a professor to whom I owe my deepest gratitude. That professor, sadly no longer here to celebrate the book's publication, was Donald H. Juel. In his likely manner, Dr. Juel said that for the final paper in his class we could write about anything as long it was on God and as long as it was interesting. I wrote a paper on the metaphor of the God who feeds in Luke 12 and investigated the Old Testament and postbiblical interpretative context of this text. As so often happens, by chance, I stumbled on a Dutch work, *Brood uit De Hemel*, which referred to the rabbinic interpretation of the manna tradition, where an image of a mother nursing her child is used to describe God's provision of food. This planted the seed for the study that would become my PhD dissertation and later be expanded to form *The God Who Provides*. Although Dr. Juel passed away much too soon, I and everyone who knew him find consolation in the fact that his inspiration lives on in many of his students and colleagues. This book, dedicated to his memory, is tangible evidence of his continuing presence.

I want to thank all the people who read *The God Who Provides* in its many different stages, from seminar paper, to dissertation, to completed manuscript. I also want to express my deepest gratitude to my dissertation committee, Dennis T. Olson, Katharine Doob Sakenfeld, and Donald H. Juel, who brought their unique perspectives to my work. I cannot begin to describe how much I have learned from these remarkable teachers and mentors. I do know that, in many ways, I model my research and teaching career on the wonderful examples they provide. In addition, I want to thank Patrick D. Miller and Walter Brueggemann for their willingness to read drafts of *The God Who Provides*. Because of their insightful comments and careful editing, this work is stronger. I also value the friendship and contributions of Matt Skinner and Eunny Lee, who attended graduate school at Princeton Theological Seminary with me. They saw this project develop from a humble semester paper to a successfully defended dissertation. I am deeply grateful for their support over the years. Matt Skinner's assistance in the area of New Testament interpretation was especially vital.

I want to thank Princeton Theological Seminary for the wonderful opportunities it offered me to grow and mature as a scholar. Particularly, as an international student, I found the financial aid and nurturing individuals essential in order to earn my PhD degree and then to find teaching and research opportunities.

The God Who Provides, moreover, has Greg Glover to thank for its existence, who, on Katharine Doob Sakenfeld's recommendation, saw the potential of the book and helped move it from dissertation to a broader, more accessible project.

I am deeply thankful to be part of the collegial and caring community of St. Norbert College, Green Bay. I thank my colleagues at St. Norbert College for their genuine excitement about this project and their encouragement to see this through. I especially want to thank Tom Bolin, Tom Reynolds, and Laurie MacDiarmid for enthusiastically reading my work. I also appreciate the generous financial assistance from the Faculty Development Fund, which allowed me to spend a summer writing in South Africa.

Finally, I want to express my deepest thanks to friends and family on both sides of the Atlantic Ocean—the many good friends I have made in the United States as well as old friends in South Africa. It is not easy to move between worlds, but your heartfelt love and support have made it doable. I especially want to thank my parents, Gys and Annette Mostert, who have always believed in me. A special word of thanks goes to my mother, who provided an exceptional model for imagining God as Mother. Finally, I want to thank Robert Vosloo, whose friendship and love proved vital in the completion of this book. Robert, I will always remember the beautiful spots we visited together, where much of this book was written, and where I ran my ideas past you over infinite cups of coffee.

LIST OF ABBREVIATIONS

1QSa	*Rule of the Congregation* (Appendix a to 1QS)
AB	Anchor Bible
ANF	*Ante-Nicene Fathers*
AT	Author's Translation
b. Ketub.	Babylonian *Ketubbot*
b. Soṭah	Babylonian *Soṭah*
b. Yoma	Babylonian *Yoma*
BEM	"Baptism, Eucharist, Ministry" (Faith and Order Paper 111; Geneva: World Council of Churches, 1982)
BibInt	*Biblical Interpretation*
BJS	Brown Judaic Studies
BR	*Biblical Research*
Cant. Rab.	*Canticles Rabbah*
Det.	*Quod deterius potiori insidari soleat [That the Worse Attacks the Better]*
Eccl. Rab.	*Ecclesiastes Rabbah*
ETL	*Ephemerides theologicae lovanienses*
ExAud	*Ex auditu*
Exod. Rab.	*Exodus Rabbah*
Gen. Rab.	*Genesis Rabbah*
Hermeneia	Hermeneia: A Critical and Historical Commentary on the Bible
IBC	Interpretation: A Bible Commentary for Teaching and Preaching
ITC	International Theological Commentary
JBL	*Journal of Biblical Literature*
JJS	*Journal of Jewish Studies*
JNSL	*Journal of Northwest Semitic Languages*
JRT	*Journal of Religious Thought*

JSNTSup	Journal for the Study of the New Testament: Supplement Series
JSOT	*Journal for the Study of the Old Testament*
JSOTSup	Journal for the Study of the Old Testament: Supplement Series
LCL	Loeb Classical Library
Leg.	*Legum allegoriae (Allegorical Interpretation)*
Lev. Rab.	*Leviticus Rabbah*
LXX	Septuagint
Mek.	*Mekilta*
Midr.	*Midrash*
MT	Masoretic Text
NICOT	New International Commentary on the Old Testament
NIDOTTE	*New International Dictionary of Old Testament Theology and Exegesis*
Num. Rab.	*Numbers Rabbah*
OBT	Overtures to Biblical Theology
Odes Sol.	*Odes of Solomon*
OTL	Old Testament Library
OTP	*Old Testament Pseudepigraha.* Edited by James H. Charlesworth. 2 vols. New York, 1983
Paed.	*Paedagogus [Christ the Educator]*
Pesiq. Rab.	*Pesiqta Rabbati*
Pesiq. Rab Kah.	*Pesiqta de Rab Kahana*
Proof	*Prooftexts: A Journal of Jewish Literary History*
PSB	*Princeton Seminary Bulletin*
RB	*Revue Biblique*
RefLitM	*Reformed Liturgy and Music*
Relig. Life	*Religion in Life*
SBL	Society of Biblical Literature
SBLDS	Society of Biblical Literature Dissertation Series
SBS	Stuttgarter Bibelstudien
Sifre Deut.	*Sifre Deuteronomy*
Sifre Num.	*Sifre Numbers*
SJT	*Scottish Journal of Theology*

TDOT	*Theological Dictionary of the Old Testament.* Edited by G. J. Botterweck and H. Ringgren. Translated by J. T. Willis, G. W. Bromiley, and D. E. Green. 8 vols. Grand Rapids, 1974–
Tg. Isa.	*Targum Isaiah*
Tg. Song.	*Targum Song of Songs*
WBC	Word Biblical Commentary
ZTK	*Zeitschrift für Theologie und Kirche*

INTRODUCTION

> Guide me, O Thou great Jehovah,
> Pilgrim through this barren land;
> I am weak, but Thou art mighty;
> Hold me with Thy powerful hand;
> Bread of heaven, Bread of heaven,
> Feed me till I want no more.
> (William Williams, 1745)[1]

The words of this familiar Christian hymn depict life as a journey through the wilderness. In wonderful biblical imagery, the hymn calls upon God's guiding presence throughout this journey. In the first stanza, God's presence is especially realized by the gift of food. Addressed by the title "Bread of heaven," referring to the divine gift of manna, God is asked to "feed me till I want no more."

At the heart of the first stanza is the metaphor of the God who feeds. It is the metaphor of the God who provided manna for Israel in the wilderness on the way to the promised land. This metaphor had ongoing significance in the Jewish and Christian religious imagination and was repeatedly employed to describe subsequent generations' experience of God.

Every time believers sing this hymn in Christian worship today, the metaphor of God's provision of food is evoked once more. Worshipers who take these words to heart may be thinking of their own personal journey through life, finding solace and comfort in the thought of God's provision in the daily routines and challenges of their lives.

The fact that this hymn is often sung during the Eucharist attests, moreover, to the fact that this metaphor for God has found its way into the practices of the church. Through reflection and formal (liturgical) use, the metaphor has become a symbol that calls to mind the world that Scripture imagines by embodying it in a simple piece of bread and a sip of wine. The words of the hymn are reinforced by the visual symbol of the bread, making the promise of God's provision real and personal.

In Jewish table blessings, this metaphor is central when God's provision of food is praised at the beginning of the "Grace after meals" (*birkat hammāzôn*):

> Blessed art Thou, O Lord, our God, King of the Universe, Who feedest the whole world with goodness, with grace and with mercy. Blessed art Thou, O Lord, who feedest all.[2]

These contemporary manifestations of the metaphor of the God who feeds illustrate something of the power of metaphors to function in people's religious imagination. Paul Avis is right when he says that Christian (and I would add Jewish) faith lives from the imagination. The Bible speaks the language of imagination and articulates beliefs about God and the world's relationship to God in metaphor, symbol, and myth. And as Brian Wren has suggested, the best metaphors are those that move us deeply by appealing to our senses and imagination.[3]

This book deals with a metaphor that has deeply moved people throughout the centuries and that has appealed to countless generations' senses and imagination. The memory of God's provision in the wilderness proved formative in Israel's religious imagination. However, an investigation of other biblical texts confirms that this metaphor of the God who feeds was a vibrant and lively metaphor that found expression in a variety of contexts. We will see how the metaphor grew and changed in meaning and how, throughout the diverse literature of the Old Testament, it maintained its significance.[4] The continuing influence of this metaphor in the postbiblical period, its presence in the New Testament, and its continual use by interpreters throughout the ages confirm the central importance of the metaphor of the God who feeds.

I argue that the metaphor of the God who feeds is one such metaphor that has the power to lure us into the world it imagines and to shape the way we view God and life in the world. Using this metaphor today, though, raises some questions. How ought one to talk about the God who feeds in a consumer society that is overfed? Or in a world where millions of people still experience starvation? We will reflect on these questions and more as we ponder the relevance of the metaphor of the God who feeds for our time.

And what about the gender of the God who feeds? Is it important? When people think of the metaphor of a God who provides food, many may have an image of a male God in mind. As Elizabeth Johnson notes, in "Western art the most common depiction of deity is that of an old white man with a white beard."[5] Thus, one could say that if people only see male imagery and only hear male metaphors, like king, ruling lord, or father, to describe God, they will tend to perceive a neutral metaphor such as the God who feeds as male.

In contrast, this book will depict the metaphor of the God who feeds differently. Theologians such as Sallie McFague argue that the symbols of food and feeding have always been closely related to women's experience. Women's bodies have the capacity to sustain the new life they bring forth. Especially in antiquity, a child did not live unless a woman nursed it at her breast. Consequently, the act of providing food to the young, especially nursing, constitutes a significant part of women's experience.[6] Aside from nursing, Kim Chernin eloquently formulates the connection between women and food.

> For food, in fact, preserves the silenced history of women's power. From infancy and through all the stages of our later development, women have exhibited in their relation to food capacities and qualities they have surrendered in many other aspects of their lives. Adept at the mysteries of creating bread from a cup of water, a handful of flour, a pinch of salt, a woman serves up the loaf that is the bread of life—exhibiting in the bowls and retorts of her domestic alchemy the awesome power of transforming matter into nurturance. Skilled in the preparation of those healing infusions of chamomile tea to relieve a belly ache, soft gelatin for a flu, cranberries without sugar to help with nausea, she all along was the mother-magician, adept at the healing arts.[7]

This introduces one of the key concerns in feminist biblical interpretation, namely, the notion of inclusive language for God.[8] Feminist theologians strongly challenge the assumption that God is strictly a male God. For example, Elizabeth Johnson argues that the mystery of who God is includes the truth that both male and female are created in the image of God so that both male and female may point to God. Actually, in the biblical traditions, we find numerous male *and* female, animate and inanimate images to describe God: God is said to be a rock, leopard, bear, eagle, potter, builder, farmer, midwife, woman in labor, king, husband, father, shepherd, and warrior. The multitude of images suggests the recognition of the biblical writers that no one image could adequately capture the "I AM WHO I AM" (Exod 3:14). To lift up female imagery alongside the more well-known male imagery for God is important as it has the effect of shattering the exclusivity of the male metaphors. Female metaphors for God, which often arise from the concrete challenges and joys that women experience, offer new ways of speaking about God, therefore leading to "a greater sense of the mystery of God."[9] Inclusive language thus enriches rather than diminishes our understanding of our relationship with God.

Employing biblical material in a study such as this, of course, presents the challenge of how to deal with the patriarchal nature of the text. Several feminists challenge the idea that biblical traditions *can be* reclaimed and reinterpreted for women. Other feminists still have not relinquished the hope of creatively employing biblical texts. Many follow some sort of revisionary or compensatory approach.[10] There are various manifestations of this approach, from endeavors focusing on the strong women characters in the biblical stories to reclaiming the female imagery for God.[11] With regard to women characters, Rita Nakashima Brock notes: "There was a problem, however, that emerged as this phase of active research on women flourished. No matter how hard we searched and no matter how far we looked, there were not enough women to balance the male-dominated picture."[12] The same thing could be said for reclaiming the female imagery for God. Historically, male and female metaphors for God simply have not received equal attention in the biblical traditions or in theological language. Thus, if one includes only the texts that show explicit signs of some female presence, one's canon within the canon will be quite meager.

Although part of the present study uses a compensatory approach as it focuses on texts where female metaphors for God occur, it also moves in the direction of creatively employing texts that offer no explicit associations of God with femaleness. In an approach that Elisabeth Schüssler Fiorenza calls "imaginative identification," one "not only focuses on the women characters of biblical stories, but also imagines women characters in the so-called 'generic' stories that do not explicitly mention women but allow for their presence." This approach allows women to enter the texts by means of "historical imagination, narrative amplifications, artistic recreations" and "liturgical celebrations."[13] Thus, the reader employs various creative techniques within the text that can create a meaning that allows for women's experience. Thus the meaning of the text extends to imagine God not only as male but also as female by employing female metaphors to describe God's relation to her children.

This book develops the female associations of the metaphor of the God who feeds. We will see in chapter 1 how a number of rabbinic texts employ a female metaphor of a mother nursing her child to describe the God who feeds. In addition, two pentateuchal texts, Num 11:11-12 and Deut 32:13-16, use the same female metaphor in the context of a description of God's provision of food. I argue that such connections invite us to think of the God who feeds in maternal terms.

This book will explore some further dimensions of the metaphor of the God who feeds in the rest of the Old Testament and as it is appropriated by the New Testament. Most of these occurrences are gender neutral; thus, there are no explicit female associations with this metaphor. However, the suggestive links with female imagery in chapter 1 provide the impetus to change the way we think about the metaphor, bestowing maternal associations on the metaphor of God's provision of food. And, if one looks deeper, there are some implicit connections with female imagery that can be used to develop the female dimension of the God who feeds. Thus, in the rest of the book, I will provide some feminist theological reflections concerning the ways in which one could imaginatively develop the female associations of the God who feeds in light of the intriguing connections made in chapter 1.

Lifting up female associations of this metaphor may extend people's religious imagination and challenge them to regard the God who feeds in a new light. Furthermore, to think of this metaphor in maternal terms opens up a whole new set of possibilities. The metaphor of God's provision of food is multifaceted in nature, thereby showing the various ways in which God is like a mother to us. Ultimately, I argue that to think of God as the Mother who feeds may enrich our understanding of God's provision for God's children. My hope is that when worshipers again sing the words, "Bread of heaven, feed me till I want no more," they will embrace the richness a female understanding of the God who feeds brings.

METAPHOR AND BIBLICAL INTERPRETATION

Many volumes have been written on the theory of metaphor and metaphorical theology.[14] In recent years, studies on metaphor in biblical studies have grown in number. The work by William Brown on metaphor and the role of imagination in the Psalms and Leo Perdue's work on metaphor in the Wisdom literature are particularly formative in my own thinking.[15] Janet Soskice's definition of metaphor serves as a good point of departure. According to her, a metaphor says something that cannot be said in any other way. She defines metaphor as "speaking about one thing in terms which are seen to be suggestive of another."[16] Thus, a metaphor uses the network of associations of a subject from one's own experience (vehicle) to disclose something new about another subject that is less well known (tenor) but that still carries its own set of associations with it. These networks of associations interact in order to create a totally new meaning. One should note that as the tenor and the vehicle are inseparable, the metaphor is a unique product of the whole. Using the example of "the God who feeds," one employs the associations of the provision of food to say something new about the associations we have of God. It is also important to note that what transpires in a metaphor is not a static onetime occurrence. Paul Avis describes more accurately the fusion of the worlds of the tenor and vehicle as an event, that is, in P. N. Furbank's words, "an invitation to an activity, ending in an impossibility."[17] This sense of "impossibility" is inherent to the notion that the metaphor is not just redescribing, but disclosing a truth for the first time. We use a metaphor to say something about God that cannot be said in any other way. Thus, a metaphor is genuinely creative, as it generates new insights and may give birth to a new understanding.

Leo Perdue's description of the metaphorical process is helpful for the purpose of this study. The first stage involves some dissonance or tension, as the metaphor tends to cross traditional boundaries. However, within this ability to shock or surprise lay the seeds of new insights. This element of surprise allows people to listen afresh and is responsible for generating a new understanding. Depending on the audience's receptiveness, a second stage may occur involving a "shock of recognition" as the audience realizes that something in the relationship between the tenor and vehicle rings true. For a moment at least, the impossible has become possible. Perdue further notes that particularly compelling metaphors may reach a third stage, "transformation," where the reader's worldview is altered or even shaped anew. At this point, the reader has achieved a new understanding concerning the metaphor, which is so persuasive that it changes the way the reader thinks. If the reader alters his or her actions based on this new understanding, the final stage in the process, "restabilization," may be reached, which, according to Perdue, creates new ways of living in the world.[18]

This book will trace (or as Marc Brettler calls it, "map") the metaphor of the God who feeds throughout the biblical material as well as in a selection of postbiblical interpretations.[19] Throughout this interpretation process, I will follow a dialogical model for biblical theology. This model is inspired by the work of the Russian literary theorist Mikhail Bakhtin.[20] In my opinion, this dialogical model provides a fruitful means for exploring the metaphor of God's provision of food.

This model exhibits the following characteristics: First, as a biblical theologian, I will construe a dialogue of biblical and postbiblical voices around the metaphor of the God who feeds. A number of texts, all which display some manifestation of the metaphor of God's provision of food, will be read together. Each of these voices, as it participates in the conversation on this metaphor, brings a distinctive perspective to the discussion. This dialogue is based on the assumption that the meaning of the metaphor is not to be found in any one of these individual texts, but in the midst of the space where the texts interact. In this conversation, a meaning is generated that contributes to a new understanding of God. This insight is particularly significant in light of the female associations bestowed on this metaphor in chapter 1.

Second, within this dialogue, each text comes to the conversation with its own unique perspective, which includes attention to its particular historical and literary context. We see something of this in Bakhtin's concern that the respective voices within the dialogue are not collapsed, but retain their distinct temporal and spatial positions. Although each text's sociohistorical location will be respected, the conversation will not be dominated by historical concerns.[21] This greater emphasis on the literary and theological dimension of each text is part of a larger shift in biblical studies that regards historical criticism to be in the service of further theological reflection. As Brevard Childs argues, "The depth dimension aids in understanding the interpreted text, and does not function independently of it."[22]

As a result, each manifestation of the metaphor of God's provision of food will be investigated within the particular biblical context in which it occurs. The meaning of a metaphor depends to a great extent on the literary context in which it is found. In light of the fact that we partly receive the network of associations raised by the metaphor from the narratives and poems in which it appears, the narrative and poetic details are important, as they contribute to our understanding of the metaphor.

Third, another significant aspect of this model is that it invites the voices of Jewish and Christian interpreters to join the conversation, building on the recent appreciation in biblical studies for the voices of premodern biblical interpreters. I have argued that the role of these voices can fruitfully be described in terms of Bakhtin's concept of the "outsider," which may consist of a foreign culture or an unfamiliar text that introduces a different perspective on the conversation. These often surprising new viewpoints may indeed spark the reader's imagination, allowing him or her to read the biblical material in a fresh way.

Fourth, the world that Scripture imagines is not devoid of ambiguities and tensions. Throughout this book, we will see evidence of the negative dimension to the metaphor of God's provision of food. For instance, in chapter 3, we will encounter an important countervoice that testifies that God at times fails to feed God's children. A dialogical model for biblical theology provides the means for holding diverse and sometimes even contradictory voices in balance. In this regard, the work done by biblical theologians who have suggested that the center of the biblical witness lies in the polarities and tensions itself is significant.[23] This important perspective is based on the acknowledgment that life itself is complex and filled with contradictions. Moreover, this countervoice will help one to discover the richness and fullness of the metaphor of the God who feeds.

Fifth, we will engage in this dialogue on the metaphor of the God who feeds with the understanding that the dialogue is never quite completed. There is always more that could be said about the theme, more texts that could be introduced into the conversation, and more interpretative voices that could be consulted—a notion illustrated well by Bakhtin's argument about the unfinalizability of the dialogue. This further suggests something of the reality that no theological claim can capture God in God's entirety, that the theological imagining and reimagining of God should continue as long as there are believers to speak of God. At the same time, one realizes that, for the sake of intelligibility and clarity, one has to draw parameters within which the dialogue might take place. Accordingly, from the magnitude of biblical interpreters, I present only a few key interpretations. However, this is based on the understanding and hope that the current conversation might invite further dialogue.

Finally, within this dialogue something of the stages Leo Perdue proposes concerning the metaphorical process manifest themselves. Some elements of the metaphor of the God who feeds may at first contain something of a shock value, offering surprisingly fresh theological perspectives. However, out of this initial shock there may grow a sense of recognition, as the reader sees that this metaphor expresses something vital about God and God's relationship to the world. And, this metaphor may appeal to our senses and imagination, even shape the way we understand God and ourselves in relation to God. Or as we will see in the concluding chapter of this book, in the case of the Eucharist, this metaphor has grown into a symbol.

With this in mind, we will now begin the process of "mapping" or "unpacking" the metaphor of the God who feeds. We will see in chapter 1 how the metaphor of God's provision to Israel in the wilderness manifests itself in remarkable ways in Israel's imagination, as well as in the imagination of later biblical interpreters. As mentioned before, chapter 1 will also present examples of a female image of nursing that is employed to describe the God who feeds. In chapter 2, we will see how Israel understood all too well that God's provision of food could not be claimed solely for its own purpose but that God's care extends to all of creation. Chapter 3 will show how Israel's understanding of the causes and consequences of the exile profoundly affected the metaphor of God's provision of food. Although exhibiting some disturbing imagery of famine in which God seems to be withholding food, this chapter will provide an important counterperspective which ought to be incorporated into a mature understanding of God. In chapter 4, we will see that even in the midst of the exile, as people struggled to survive the famine, they firmly held on to the belief that God would feed again. Accordingly, God's glorious restoration of Israel's land and people is expressed in the richest food imagery imaginable. Chapter 5 will provide quite a different perspective when we will see how food imagery also plays a significant role in the image of Woman Wisdom's gifts of food. Wisdom, and her relationship to God, provides intriguing evidence for reimagining the metaphor of the God who feeds in female terms. The final chapter will offer some concluding remarks on the metaphor of God's provision of food, highlighting not only the promising elements related to this metaphor but also some of the problems associated with using it. In addition, this chapter will offer some perspectives on the New Testament trajectories of the metaphor of the God who feeds, wherein God's provision of food is concretized in the figure of Jesus. In light of this connection, we will, in conclusion, note some of the ways in which the sacrament of the Eucharist builds on the rich biblical tradition concerning the God who feeds.

CHAPTER 1

MANNA FROM HEAVEN AND MOTHER'S MILK

Reimagining the Metaphor of God's Provision of Food for Israel

Central to Israel's understanding of the metaphor of the God who feeds is the narrative that tells of God's provision of manna and quail to Israel. Different versions of this story are told in Exod 16 and Num 11. In Exod 16, we read how Israel complains bitterly to Moses and Aaron about their fear of dying of hunger in the wilderness. The Israelites remember the "good life" in Egypt where they had plenty of food to eat (v. 3). Now, they are just hungry and in desperate need of food. God fulfills exactly this need by sending the quail in the evening and manna in the morning. It seems as if the quail play a minor role in this narrative, occurring only in verse 13. However, the manna becomes in this narrative and in later interpretations the essential symbol of God's providence. In Num 11, we find Israel complaining again. This time not because they are hungry, but because they are bored with the manna. Again God listens to their cries and sends them quail to eat. But as we will see later, there is a twist to the story.[1]

God's provision of food to Israel is quite significant for Israel's understanding of their relationship with God. This is evident from the repeated reference to manna in the rest of the Old Testament. For instance, Neh 9:15 says that God gave Israel bread from heaven to feed their hunger.

This continues in Neh 9:20-21 where God did not withhold manna from Israel. God sustained Israel in the wilderness for forty years so that they lacked nothing (לא חסרו). Also in Ps 78:24-25, God rained down manna on them to eat, which is lyrically called "grain of heaven" and "bread of angels."

In addition, throughout the centuries, God's gracious gift to Israel has captured interpreters' imaginations such that it has been the inspiration for innovative theological reflection. One of the most intriguing moves was made by rabbis who introduced creative imagery to describe manna and its significance. For instance, several texts make a connection between manna or food imagery and nursing imagery when nursing language is used to describe God's provisional care. It seems they thought that the metaphor of a mother nursing her baby provided a fitting description of God's complete care in the wilderness, expressing the fullness of life people experienced during this time. A baby drinks every day from the mother's breast, which completely satisfies his or her nutritional needs. Similarly, every day Israel had enough manna to eat in the wilderness and was completely dependent on God's protection. What better way to express this absolute reliance on God for food than the relationship of a child with his or her mother?[2] One sees a good example of this type of interpretation in *b. Yoma 75a*, one of the Jewish (or rabbinic) writings of the Babylonian Talmud, which contains some interesting exegetical comments on biblical texts in the midst of a running commentary on the Mishnah (Jewish legal material).[3] As so often happens in rabbinic interpretation, this midrash[4] grows out of an exegetical problem, such as a word that does not fit its context, an unusual word or unusual spelling of a word, or inconsistencies between biblical traditions. James Kugel uses the following illustration to explain: "the text's irregularity is the grain of sand which so irritates the midrashic oyster that he constructs a pearl around it."[5]

The problem that caught the attention of the rabbis is that the biblical text contains diverse opinions on how the manna tasted. Exodus 16:31 says that the manna tastes like "wafers made with honey," while Num 11:8 says that manna tastes like "cakes baked with oil." One solution for this problem was an interpretation that argued that the manna had a variety of tastes. For example, Rabbi Ishmael says in the *Mekilta de-Rabbi Ishmael*, "Moses said to Jethro: 'In this manna which God has given to us, we can taste the taste of bread, the taste of meat, the taste of fish, the taste of locust, and the taste of all the delicacies in the world.'"[6]

The notion of the variety of tastes of the manna forms the basis for the interpretation in *b. Yoma 75a*, which connects manna with nursing imagery by means of a clever play on words in the exposition of Num 11:8 (italics represent a quotation within a quotation): "*And the taste of it was as the taste of a cake baked with oil* (Num 11:8). R. Abbuha said: [Do not read *le-shad* (לשד 'cake'), but *shad* (שד 'breast') viz:].[7] Just as the infant (תינוק) finds many a flavour at the breast (שד), so also did Israel find many a taste in the manna as long as they were eating it."[8]

B. *Yoma* makes a connection between the word for breast (שַׁד) and the word for cakes (לְשַׁד) in Num 11:8—the latter whose meaning is not entirely clear. This connection builds on the fact that a mother's milk has a variety of tastes, depending on the types of food the mother has eaten. This notion of the variety in tastes of manna corresponds to the basic understanding of the sufficiency of God's care. Just as God provided a variety of tastes of manna, so God provides in a special way for the unique needs of each of God's children.

One finds another example of this type of interpretation in the rabbinic commentary (midrash) on the book of Numbers, *Sifre Num.* 89, which uses the metaphor of a nursing infant as illustration of the significance of manna:

> D. Another explanation for the statement, ". . . and the taste of it was like the taste of cakes baked with oil:" just as for an infant [תינוק] the teat [דד] is the main thing and everything else is secondary, so the manna was the main thing for the Israelites and everything else was secondary to it.
>
> E. Another explanation: just as in the case of a teat even though an infant may suck on it all day long, he does not do any harm to it, so in the case of manna, even though the Israelites ate it all day long, it did not do them any harm.
>
> F. Another explanation: just as in the case of a teat, it is really only one thing but [for the infant] it turns into many things, so the manna turned for Israelites into everything they could imagine. It may be compared to saying to a woman, "Do not eat garlic or onions on account of the infant."
>
> G. Another explanation: just as in the case of the teat, the infant is pained when he has to give it up, so the Israelites were pained when they had to give up the manna, as it is said: "And the manna ceased on the next day" (Joshua 5:12).[9]

Sifre Numbers 89 draws an extended analogy between the "teat" or "breast/nipple" and the manna. The image of a mother nursing her child becomes a powerful way to describe God's complete care for the children of Israel as evidenced in the provision of manna in the wilderness. This even though the interpretation indicates that the writer probably had no experience nursing. For instance, as any new mother can tell, the reference to the infant doing no harm is not necessarily true. The mother is often sore, especially when the child's teeth start coming in.

A third text that also describes God's care by means of nursing language is an interesting midrash on Exod 1:12 found in *Exod. Rab.* 1:12 and *b. Soṭah 11b*. This interpretation appears in a narrative where Pharaoh is doing his best to prevent Israel from procreating. The midrash notices a problem regarding the promise God made to Abraham. Did God not promise Abraham that God would multiply Abraham's children like the stars of the heaven? What is more, Exod 1:12 says that "the more they were oppressed, the more they multiplied." In order to solve this difficulty, *Exod. Rab.* tells the following story of how it happened that the people of Israel became a great nation.

The basic assumption of this text is that it had to be God's miraculous intervention and care which allowed Israel to flourish despite their difficult circumstances. So, God aided the Israelite women in creating circumstances in which they were able to conceive. Second, when the babies were born, God sent someone (*Exod. Rab.* has an angel) to act as a midwife and cleanse and beautify the newborns. Third, we read, "He then provided for them two balls [breast-shaped rocks, עגולין], one made of oil [שמן] and the other of honey [דבש], as it is said: *And He made him to suck* [ויניקהו] *honey out of the crag, and oil out of the flinty rock* (Deut xxxii, 13)."[10] (Italics represent a quotation within a quotation.)

We see in this text how God provided nourishment for the babies by providing a substitute for mother's milk. Using the prooftext of Deut 32:13 as basis, this interpretation says that God nursed the babies with honey and oil.

The rabbis did not pull this innovative interpretation out of thin air. At the heart of these interpretations are two biblical texts, Deut 32:13 and Num 11:11-12, which use a similar female metaphor of nursing (the verb ינק) to describe God's provision of food to Israel.

Deuteronomy 32:13-14 uses this striking metaphor in the context of food imagery to describe God's care for Israel:

> [God] set [Israel] atop the heights of the land,
>> and fed him with produce of the field;
> [God] nursed [יֵנִק] him with honey from the
>> crags [דְּבַשׁ מִסֶּלַע],
>> with oil from flinty rock [וְשֶׁמֶן מֵחַלְמִישׁ צוּר];
> curds from the herd, and milk from the flock,
>> with fat of lambs and rams;
> Bashan bulls and goats,
>> together with the choicest wheat—
>> you drank fine wine from the blood of grapes.

This metaphor of God nursing Israel is part of a detailed portrayal of God in the Song of Moses, describing God's care for Israel. In the first part of the song (vv. 4-14), a series of metaphors draw a dramatic picture of the faithful God. God is a Rock (v. 4), an Eagle (v. 11), culminating in the vivid description of God feeding and nursing God's children (vv. 13-14). While verse 13*a* says "God caused Israel to ride on the heights of the land and fed it with products of the field" (AT), there is some confusion whether this provision refers to the time in the wilderness or in the promised land. However, as poetic language does not always have one clear referent, verse 13 may actually be a transitional verse. One could then say that God's care extends through the wilderness into the promised land (cf. Josh 5:11-12 where it says that "the manna ceased on the day they ate the produce of the land"). God's care in terms of feeding surely reached a climax in the gift of manna Israel received from God in the wilderness. However, God continued to provide nutrition once Israel reached the promised land. Deuteronomy 8:7-10 states that it is God who brought Israel into the good land, a land of plenty where the Israelites were able to eat more than enough. It is no coincidence that the promised land is also described in terms of food imagery, namely, a land of milk and honey (Exod 3:17; 13:5; 33:3; Num 13:27; 14:8; 16:13; Deut 6:3; 11:9; 26:9, 15; 27:3; 31:20; Josh 5:6).[11]

In the midst of the food imagery, one finds the female metaphor of God nursing (יָנַק) Israel "with honey from the crags, / with oil from flinty rock." The term *to nurse* points to the absolute reliance of a baby on his or her mother as well as the absolute sufficiency of the provision. Also, the terms honey and oil serve to emphasize God's amazing care for Israel. Both *honey* and *oil* were regarded as Middle Eastern staples.[12] Particularly oil had a multipurpose value, being used for food (1 Kgs 17:12), cosmetics (Eccl 9:7-8), fuel for lamps (Exod 25:6), and medicine (Isa 1:6). Oil thus served as testimony of God's blessing. The fact that both oil and honey could be produced without human cultivation contributed to the development of oil and honey as symbols of God's care for the people of Israel.[13]

The metaphor of God nursing Israel continues in the rich food imagery in verse 14. Important to note is that all the gifts in verse 14, which are all foods of the best kind, are included under the verb "to nurse" (יָנַק), attesting to the central role that nursing imagery plays within the broader context of food imagery. Thus, God is not only nursing Israel with honey and oil but also with abundant foods cited in rapid succession. As Johanna W. H. Van Wijk-Bos notes, "The poet seems unable to stop, piling one symbol of abundant sustenance on top of another: honey, oil, milk, butter, fat, and wine are all provided."[14]

A second text, which uses a female metaphor of nursing to describe God's care, is in Num 11:11-15. In this text, Moses delivers a strong appeal where he basically offers his resignation as nurse. In a series of rhetorical questions, Moses asks whether he has conceived (הרה) and given birth (ילד) to these children so that he should be assigned the duties of a nurse (הָאֹמֵן), carrying the nursing child (הַיֹּנֵק) in her bosom (v. 12).[15] Moses knows that they are on their way to a land of plenty, the promised land of milk and honey (e.g., Exod 3:8, 17; 13:5; Lev 20:24; Num 13:2). But in the meantime, while journeying through the wilderness, somebody has to provide food for the "infants." In anguish, Moses angrily asks where *he* is supposed to find meat for Israel to eat. Moses expresses his utter inability to provide for the people's wants, saying in verse 14 that he is not able to carry these people alone, for they are too heavy for him. In conclusion, Moses insists that God is mistreating him and that God should either change his situation or kill him (v. 15).

Moses views himself as the substitute mother or wet nurse for God's children, implying that God is not fulfilling his duties as Mother. In the ancient Near East, wet nurses were brought in if a mother was unable to nurse, if she did not have enough milk, or if she had died.[16] Moses urges God, whom he considers to be the real Mother, to step in and fulfill God's maternal duties by providing food and care.

Moses' speech arises from his misunderstanding of his own role in relationship to the people, when he takes the burden of caring for them solely onto himself. Moses does not fully grasp that God *has* been providing food to the infant Israel all along. And Israel also does not recognize God's care for what it is. Israel has begun to take for granted this daily nutrition, which, like a mother's breast milk, is always there and always enough. In verse 6, Israel complains that the tediousness of the manna parallels the dryness of its existence—this in contrast to the manna, which according to the narrator had many uses, tasted like "cakes made with oil" (v. 8), and came with the dew (v. 9). Thus, although Israel and Moses both are at fault in not recognizing God's care, Num 11 emphasizes that God's care is indeed more than sufficient. This narrative portrays God as the One who functions as the Mother, the One who "nurses" Israel by providing food enough for each day. Manna is versatile and sufficient, nourishing to the body as dew is nourishing to the vegetation. By using nursing imagery in the context of the manna narrative, the absolute sufficiency of God's care is highlighted. The narrative emphasizes that Moses does not have to be the wet nurse to the people, as God's "milk" is enough for the people. Moses does not need to provide food, since God is already fulfilling this function.

This explicitly female metaphor, which is to be found in Deut 32 and Num 11, encourages the reader to imagine God's provision of food for Israel in terms of a mother nursing her children. Many years ago these same texts caused rabbis to come up with a similar interpretation, giving rise to some of the beautiful interpretations we have encountered in the beginning of this chapter.

Then again, we have to realize that the female metaphor of nursing that is used to describe God's provision, occurs only in a few instances. Most of the other texts referring to God's provision of food to Israel in the form of manna, for example, Ps 78:24-25; Deut 8:3; Neh 9:15, 20-21; and most notably Exod 16, do not employ a female metaphor and can be considered gender neutral. However, the instances that do use a female metaphor provide suggestive evidence that encourages and enriches our understanding of a God who feeds in maternal terms. Thus, whereas some people's natural inclination would be to hear the metaphor of the God who feeds in Exod 16 and other texts dealing with God's provision of food in male terms, the interaction with texts like Num 11 and Deut 32, as well as the connotations left by the voices of the postbiblical interpreters, opens up our imagination to other possibilities. As a result, when one reads, for instance, in Exod 16 the description of God's amazing care for Israel in the form of manna, the metaphor of a mother nursing her child may be a fruitful way to view God's care. With this in mind, let us take a fresh look at God's provision of food in Exod 16.

In Exod 16, God's care for her children is illustrated by a number of special characteristics. The manna is said to be "bread from heaven" (Exod 16:4) in contrast to the bread from the earth that is cultivated by human hands. Moreover, manna is said to "rain down" in verse 4. Instead of sending rain to water grains, God bypasses farming and directly rains down "bread." Finally, God's provision of the daily bread is like clockwork, as the manna is said to be there every morning.

Manna is part of three miracles. The miraculous nature of manna serves the function of describing God's care in the most magnificent terms. In the first miracle, the people find that the manna they have gathered is equal in amount for each person. Although the people gathered more or less, each person had exactly the same when they measured it. This is reinforced when verse 18 states that nobody lacked anything (cf. also the same word that is used in Ps 23:1 and Deut 2:7). The manna thus satisfied their needs perfectly. The second miracle is that manna is only found six days a week and not on the Sabbath. After Moses instructed Israel concerning this Sabbath regulation, some people still went out to find manna on the Sabbath, but they could not find any (vv. 25-27). The rhythm of fresh manna each morning is broken one day a week, emphasizing that God makes special arrangements for a special day. When the people gathered manna on the sixth day, they saw that they had gathered a double portion (v. 22). Thus, miraculously, the manna is not only enough for their usual daily ration but also for the extra day of rest.

The third miracle is that, in contrast to the other days in which manna could not be stored successfully, the extra manna for the Sabbath does not go foul. Verse 23 suggests that the people should prepare the manna on the sixth day in whichever way they desire, and what is left over, they should keep for the Sabbath. Whereas on the other days the leftover manna grew contaminated with worms, and thereby prevented Israel from storing manna for the next day, the usual rhythm is once more sidestepped in order to make special provision for the Sabbath.

These last two miracles relate to an added feature of God's amazing care for Israel. God provides a day of rest for the people on the Sabbath. Thus, especially on the Sabbath, Israel experiences God's care and its reliance on God. The reason for this is that God is not only providing a day of rest for God's children, but also miraculously ensures that this rest does not occur at the expense of their daily needs.

The miraculous character of the manna contributes to the notion of living each day in expectation of only that day's food. Israel was not able to secure their future through collecting and saving. In the wilderness, Israel's only option was to trust God fully for each day's food and thus be totally reliant on God.

The experience of life in the wilderness, with only God to rely on for food and security, might be why other interpretations employ a metaphor of a mother and child to describe this profound theological claim. A metaphor of a mother nursing her child is a fitting illustration to describe God's daily provision of food, which is always there and always enough. The reason for this is that the trust and reliance that Israel is supposed to demonstrate is illustrated well by the metaphor of a baby—a baby who is totally reliant on his or her mother for food and care.

If one uses this illustration to describe God's care, we could say that God is depicted in Exod 16 as the caring Mother, who makes certain that her children are fed every day. She ensures that there is enough for each child, that no one goes hungry. And in Exod 16, the remarkable care of God for her children is illustrated in the most magnificent terms, as seen in the special characteristics attributed to the manna, as well as the various miracles the manna is said to be a part of. Moreover, in her special way, God not only ensures that everybody has enough food to eat but also recognizes that enough rest is equally important for the upkeep of our bodies. Thus, a sign of God's special care for her children is that she creates spaces for them to rest and recuperate.

Thus far, we have seen how the maternal dimension of the metaphor of the God who feeds predominantly described God's amazing and sometimes even miraculous care for Israel. Although this meaning is surely the most important connotation associated with this metaphor, there are more dimensions to it. In a close reading of the pentateuchal narratives as well as in the rabbinic interpretations of these texts, it becomes clear that the metaphor of God's provision of food exhibits multiple dimensions, thereby bestowing a rich perspective on God's love for the people. These dimensions should be kept in view as they provide glimpses of how Israel perceived God. Moreover, these dimensions contribute to a picture of God as a Mother of great versatility.[17]

A MOTHER OF GREAT VERSATILITY

Listening to Her Children

A significant part of God's provision of food to Israel is that it represents God's attentive nature. This dimension of the metaphor of the God who feeds is closely associated with the notion of God's presence. In the wilderness traditions, food (and water) is regarded as a sure sign of God's presence. Thus, God's actions of providing food in response to Israel's cries contribute to Israel's understanding that God is with them. God's presence is further depicted in Exod 16 when the repeated reference to the glory of God (vv. 7, 10), which is closely associated with God's provision of the substance necessary for human life, is used as a symbol of God being in the midst of Israel.

Moreover, we see in both Num 11 and Exod 16 how God, time and again, hears Israel's cries (e.g., Exod 16:7, 8, 9, 12; Num 11:1-3, 20). In both of these stories, God responds markedly, albeit in different ways. For instance, in Exod 16, God replies to Israel's complaints by giving Israel precisely what they requested. Accordingly, God promises to give Israel bread to satisfy their hunger and meat like they had to eat in Egypt, and then later in the narrative fulfills this promise. In Num 11, however, God's response looks a little different. God indeed acknowledges Israel's dissatisfaction with the food, and responds by coming down (ירד vv. 17, 25). This action of God has the effect of bridging the distance between above and below, thereby making Godself accessible to God's people.[18] Then in response to Israel's complaints and Moses' challenge that God is not fulfilling God's maternal duties (vv. 11-15), God makes a point of showing that God is more than able to provide for Israel's needs, by giving Israel exactly what they asked for: meat and more meat (vv. 18-20). Although the food initially seems to be a blessing, ironically, one later sees how the signs of destruction are already to be found in the food. Nevertheless, the fact that God responds, even though by punishment, shows that God does listen.

Continuing the process of reimagining God in female terms, God is portrayed in Exod 16 and Num 11 as an attentive Mother who overhears Israel's murmurings, who listens carefully to her children's complaints and takes them seriously. As Mother, God is said to be near to Israel in the act of providing food, this being a manifestation of God's glory. Moreover, God voluntarily responds to Israel's needs by providing her children exactly what they requested—this even though there is an element of punishment embedded in God's provision of food. Nevertheless, one could say that God pays close attention to God's children and that even God's discipline is an act of love.

Punishing Those Whom She Loves

In the previous dimension, we have seen indications that the metaphor of the God who feeds not only is a positive metaphor but also contains a strong dimension of punishment. This is evident in Num 11, where God's anger concerning the Israelites' craving for meat is described in vivid terms (Num 11:1, 10, 33). God is furious that even though the people have manna to eat they "crave" (אוה) for more. The problem with Israel is that they are remembering the wrong things. Instead of remembering God and God's deliverance from Egypt, they hark back to Egypt and Egypt's foods (v. 5). Israel thus fails to regard the manna they receive as a daily blessing, coming from God. By rejecting the food, Israel rejects God by showing a lack of trust in the power of God.

So God punishes God's children by providing food in abundance (vv. 19-20, 31).[19] God provides Israel plenty of meat to eat in the form of quail, which fell all around the camp, a day's journey to either end, about two cubits deep (v. 31). However, there is an ambiguity in this abundance. At first it seems as if the reference to quail and its duration for a month (vv. 18-20) is a positive element, a gracious response by a gracious God to the needs of God's children. But, the second part of verse 20 shows the opposite to be true when it says that the people will eat from the quail "until [the meat] comes out of your nostrils and becomes loathsome to you." This is the first sign that the abundance of the food might be intended as punishment. Verse 33 shows that while eating, disaster strikes and the Israelites become gravely ill. Thus, one sees that the signs of destruction are already present in the food. Especially telling is the contrast between the daily bread, just enough for each day, and the overabundance of the quail, which has disastrous effects in the end.

This dark motif of Israel's apostasy and God's judgment is also illustrated in Deut 32. In the second part of the Song of Moses, we find the metaphor of God as a vengeful warrior—indeed a most troubling metaphor for modern readers.[20] Within this portrayal, we see how God will afflict God's people with evil and the arrows of pestilence and famine (vv. 22-27). In this portrayal of God as disciplinarian, food imagery again plays an intricate part. In the portrayal of God's judgment, the signs of destruction are already found in the food. The rich blessing of food is turned upside down and becomes a curse.[21] For instance, the same fat that once was the sign of God the Rock's blessing becomes the means whereby the other gods, the other rocks, are venerated with fat offerings (vv. 37-38). And the oil, which was used literally in verse 13, returns figuratively in verse 15 where "to grow fat" is used negatively in the second sense. By eating all this rich food, Israel themselves grew fat, making themselves sick with food.

The dual meaning of these words underlines the fact that abundance has a twofold function. First, it is used to describe God's goodness. In verse 13, we have shown how the nursing imagery, coupled with the extravagant, rich variety of foods as object of the nursing, served the function of emphasizing God's amazing care. Second, this same abundance contributes, though, to Israel's forgetfulness. The food that once served as a blessing and provided the nourishment necessary for life now leads to obesity and, with that, amnesia. When Israel had to look daily to God for their food, they remembered God's goodness. It is when Israel had so much to eat that they forgot to recognize God behind every blessing. The danger of abundance is that prosperous people forget the Giftgiver and think that they did it all by themselves.

We see that the portrayal of God as nurturing parent is enhanced by the metaphor of God as warrior, the One who punishes the rebellious child. One may call this the dimension of God as disciplinarian.[22] The juxtaposition of these images points to the fact that both these metaphors are necessary as they provide a balanced view of God. Moreover, thinking of these two metaphors together is not foreign to Deuteronomy. Deuteronomy 8:5 says, "Know then in your heart that as a parent disciplines a child so the LORD your God disciplines you."

The implication of this dimension is that the portrayal of God as nurturing Mother is enhanced by the dimension of God as disciplinarian in that an integral part of parenting is to exercise discipline. To think of God as a Mother disciplining her children contributes to the notion that mothers are also responsible for discipline. Such an understanding may help break down the often-heard phrase, "just wait until your father gets home." On the other hand, we will see in chapter 3 the problems associated with food being used as punishment.

Managing Her Household

In Exod 16, one finds the unique perspective of the God who feeds as managing her household. In Exod 16, one of the central miracles connected to the manna is that there is no surplus and no scarcity. No matter how much the Israelites gathered, they ended up with only what they needed. Thus, there is a limit to the amount the people may gather. There is enough food if the people adhere to the distribution scheme. The implication of this miracle is that a principle of total equality is at stake. The manna is distributed in such a way that everyone receives a portion that is exactly enough to satisfy their needs. As verse 18 narrates, the Israelites lacked nothing.

This miracle makes a profound theological claim. By equally distributing manna to everyone (v. 16), God does not make any distinction between poor and rich, weak and strong. God is equally interested in each member of the community, leading to the notion that the portrayal of God as the One providing equal amounts of food for everyone could be understood in terms of God as household manager.

Regarding the larger project of reimagining God in female terms, an intriguing perspective on the gender of the household manager is provided by Carol Meyers. Meyers argues that women are the chief preparers of cooked food throughout the preindustrialized world. Meyers argues that the preparer of the food "has a lot to say about how, when, and how much food is consumed." She concludes that in a preindustrial setting "female control of food consumption would have contributed substantially to her domestic power and status."[23]

Meyers has been critiqued for a somewhat "romantic" view of women in the early history of Israel. It is questionable whether women in Israel had a better social standing because they prepared the food.[24] However, in light of the fact that women did typically fulfill the role of preparing food and allocating food resources, it is significant that God is depicted in this narrative as a household manager who not only produces the food but also allocates and distributes food equally. One should note that Meyers's observation does not prove that God must be understood as female in Exod 16. However, for the modern reader of the biblical text, this information may serve as an added incentive to think of the God who feeds in maternal terms. God is the Mother who manages her household, who makes sure that each child is fed and cared for.

One problem with this interpretation would be that God is distributing food to a whole nation in Exod 16, thus evoking a public understanding of a household manager. Moreover, the closest Old Testament parallel of a household manager distributing food is that of the male figure of Joseph, who organizes the food supplies in Gen 37–50. This distribution occurs on a national scale rather than in an individual household, thus indicating a public rather than private sphere. In response to this difficulty, one may note that, as most of the biblical material is drawn from the public rather than the private sphere, the biblical parallels will most likely be male. This is exactly why scholars like Phyllis Bird and Carol Meyers engage in women's history in order to give voice to women's experience in antiquity. Moreover, Leo Perdue argues that "much of what the Old Testament says about the character and especially the activity of God is shaped by discourse concerning the family."[25] Thus, it is possible to interpret God's provision of food for Israel in terms of a family and household context. This interpretative option is strengthened by the fact that the nursing language that is used in parallel texts suggests a household context. Accordingly, the metaphor of God distributing food is enriched if one thinks of Israel as a family who is cared for by their parent and in this case, its mother.

Finally, this dimension of God as managing her household has far broader implications, as the picture of God in Exod 16 gives rise to an alternative social reality. Walter Brueggemann argues that manna is distributed according to a principle by which "any attempt to store up . . . or monopolize this bread is doomed to failure." This is in contrast to Egypt where "empires exist by their capacity to administer and control the supply of food (cf. Gen 47:13-19)." It seems as if the distribution of the manna sets limits on "certain kinds of social power and social inequity"—an alternative social reality that is symbolized by the jar of manna. Brueggemann argues that the jar makes a statement that is "designed to shatter food monopolies, liberate hungry people from social control and destroy every social management that promotes injustice. It intends to judge and condemn every restrictive, controlling administration of food and of life."[26]

Such an understanding gives to the metaphor of a mother as household manager a far more public role, as God is the manager of the cosmos, executing social justice for all its inhabitants. Moreover, Brueggemann and Sallie McFague both make a case that this metaphor of God as household manager makes an appeal to the reader to follow God in creating a social reality that exhibits the same measures of equality and fairness.[27]

Food as Symbol of Teaching

In postbiblical literature, God's provision of food takes on a secondary meaning when food comes to signify teaching or learning. Already in Deut 8:3 one finds a connection between physical food (bread/manna) and the word of God (learning/teaching), a connection that took on a life of its own in the postbiblical period. In these texts manna comes to signify the word of God by which God teaches God's children. It is noteworthy that Israel's experience of God as the provider of food formed a key aspect for envisioning a life of learning. These connections will be further worked out in chapter 5 where we will discuss the relation between Woman Wisdom's provision of food to the God who feeds.

A particularly interesting development in the literature of early Judaism is how God's care as a nursing mother becomes a metaphor for learning. In a number of rabbinic texts, nursing imagery that is used to describe God's provision of food functions as a description of how learning should occur. A good example of this type of interpretation is found in a homiletical treatment,[28] *Pesiq. Rab Kah.* 12, where manna is linked to the divine word that is customized to each person's level of understanding.

> Moreover, said R. Jose bar R. Ḥanina, the Divine Word spoke to each and every person according to his particular capacity. And do not wonder at this. For when manna came down for Israel, each and every person tasted it in keeping with his own capacity—infants in keeping with their capacity, young men in keeping with their capacity, and old men in keeping with their capacity. Infants in keeping with their capacity: like the taste of the milk that an infant sucks [שהתינוק] from his mother's breast [בשדי אמו], so was the taste of manna to every infant, for it is said "Its taste was like the taste of rich cream" (Num. 11:8); young men according to their capacity, for of the manna they ate it is said "My bread also which I gave thee, bread, and oil, and honey" (Ezek. 16:19); and old men according to their capacity, as it is said of the manna they ate "the taste of it was like wafers made with honey" (Exod. 16:31).

In this interpretation, one sees that a connection is made between manna and nursing language. For babies manna tasted like milk (or rich cream).

This interpretation builds on the notion of the difference in tastes of the manna, which emphasizes once more the sufficiency of the manna. However, in *Pesiq. Rab Kah.* 12, the manna takes on an additional meaning when it is said that just as the manna adapts to a person's capacity, so the word comes to each person according to his or her understanding; thus God is revealing Godself in a different way to each person according to his or her own level of understanding. One finds in this text evidence that manna is understood not only as physical nutrition but also as nourishment in a spiritual sense.

Another example of this type of interpretation is to be found in the midrash on Song of Songs, *Cant. Rab.* 4:5. (Italics represent a quotation within a quotation.)

> Thy two breasts [שני שדיך]: these are Moses and Aaron. Just as the breasts [השדים] are the beauty and the ornament of a woman, so Moses and Aaron were the beauty and ornament of Israel. Just as the breasts are the charm [beauty] of a woman, so Moses and Aaron were the charm of Israel. Just as the breasts are the glory and pride of a woman, so Moses and Aaron were the glory and pride of Israel. Just as the breasts are full of milk [מלאים חלב], so Moses and Aaron filled [ממלאים] Israel with Torah. Just as whatever a woman eats helps to feed the child at the breast [התינוק אוכל ויונק מהן], so all the Torah that Moses our master learned he taught to Aaron, as it is written, *And Moses told Aaron all the words of the Lord* (Ex. IV, 28). The Rabbis say: He revealed to him the ineffable Name. Just as one breast is not greater than the other, so it was with Moses and Aaron; for it is written, *These are that Moses and Aaron* (Ex. VI, 27), and it is also written, *These are that Aaron and Moses* (*ib.* 26), showing that Moses was not greater than Aaron nor was Aaron greater than Moses in knowledge of Torah.[29]

This interpretation builds on a comparison that already has been made in the Aramaic translation of the Old Testament, that is, the *Tg. Song.* 4:5 ("Your two breasts are like two fawns, twins of a gazelle, that feed among the lilies"). In *Tg. Song.* 4:5 it was said that Moses and Aaron *fed* Israel in the wilderness with manna, fowl, and water from Miriam's well. In *Cant. Rab.* 4:5 it is said that Moses and Aaron *nursed* Israel with the Torah [filled (ממלאים)], just as a mother nurses her child with milk. Once more food is raised to a new level, becoming a symbol of learning.

This metaphor is extended at great length in *Cant. Rab.* 4:5 in a praise song for Aaron and Moses. As a mother's breast is full of milk, Aaron and Moses filled (ממלאים) Israel with Torah. This reference continues the characteristic link made between Torah and food.[30] Since Moses is associated with the giving of the Torah, it is to be expected that he is the one who nursed Israel with the Torah. However, one should note that customarily *God* is the One who is said to provide Israel with manna, quail, and water in the wilderness. And it is also *God* who gives the Torah. Thus, Moses (and Aaron) should be regarded as agents of God in providing food and the Torah. By way of inference, one could argue that God fed or nursed God's children by the agency of Moses and Aaron.

Once more these interpretations are not grasped out of thin air, but have their roots deeply embedded in the pentateuchal texts, each of which develops in some way the theme of God teaching God's children.

For instance, Deut 32 makes a connection between God's gift of food and the life that God's word brings. This is particularly evident in the emphasis the Song of Moses places on learning/teaching. Not only is teaching a dominant theme in the whole book of Deuteronomy, but particularly the Song of Moses seems to exhibit an educational function.[31] Accordingly, the Song itself claims that it should be taught. Moreover, the Song strongly emphasizes the act of hearing the word of God, which is, in verse 2, likened to rain and, accordingly, is as necessary to Israel as water is for vegetation to bring about life.

As both the water and the word come from God, one could duly describe God as the Giver of life. This is even more evident in the creation and birthing language that is used to describe God in this Song (cf. e.g., "to create" [קנה] in v. 6; "to bear" [ילד] and "to give birth" [חיל] in v. 18).[32] This Giver of life is furthermore said to give food. We have seen how nursing language is used to describe the long list of foods given to the people. Nursing language signifies a recipient who is totally dependent on his or her mother for nutrition. Without milk, the baby dies. Thus, the food God gives surely brings about life. In Deuteronomy, one finds a further development when it is said that it is not only food that gives life but also God's word. So Deut 8:3 states that God taught Israel "that one does not live by bread alone, but by all that comes from the mouth of YHWH" (AT).

This connection develops one of the key themes of Deuteronomy. Israel was meant to learn from the wilderness experience that their sustenance came from God, who is depicted as a teaching parent. Israel was given nourishment and life by God's gift of manna, but they had to realize that real life depends on the words of God. Thus, throughout the book of Deuteronomy, the writer argues that Israel will receive life by keeping the commandments and the divine instruction (Deut 4:1, 4; 5:15; 8:1, 19; 11:13-17, 21; 30:15-20).

In Num 11, we see a similar dimension of God teaching God's children when Israel has to learn to recognize God as their real Mother. Underlying the theme of being disciplined by God is the assumption that Israel did not do what was right. Israel's failure to recognize God's provision of food as a gift from above led to their punishment. The message at the heart of this narrative is that Israel had to recognize that God's provision of food is nutritious, wholesome, and more than enough. Instead of yearning for the material wealth Egypt provided, Israel had to learn to trust God's provision one day at a time. It is through the daily food that Israel had the opportunity to learn to recognize God as their real Mother, thus closely associating food with teaching.

This learning process is also at the heart of Exod 16. Israel had to learn to acknowledge YHWH as the God who brought them out of Egypt and who is still present. This is evident from the fact that God "tests" the people, whether they will "walk" in God's commandment. Throughout the narrative, the terms "to know" (ידע in vv. 6, 12, 14) and "to see" (ראה in vv. 7, 12, 15, 29, 32) are used. Both "to know" and "to see" emphasize the idea that Israel had to learn to recognize God. These instances add to the understanding that bread is not only there to feed the body but also to give life on a larger scale.

More specifically, Israel had to learn three lessons. Israel first had to learn to have complete confidence in God. Israel had to learn to be totally dependent on God for their daily needs, without securing the future by producing bread by traditional human means like plowing, sowing, harvesting, and storing.

To completely trust God for one's daily bread is not always easy to do. We see in Exod 16 a dramatic description of Israel's struggles to make this lesson their own. Through the daily discipline of picking up only enough bread for today, trusting that God would provide again for tomorrow, Israel had to learn that the God who earlier had liberated them from Egypt will continue to provide in their daily needs.

One sees something of this understanding reflected in the bread petition of the Lord's Prayer (Luke 11:3). The daily sufficiency of the manna in the wilderness calls to mind the prayer: "Give us each day our daily bread," or as Joseph Fitzmeyer calls it "our essential bread."[33] This prayer beautifully expresses the trust that God will provide—a trust that has to be renewed daily.

Second, Israel had to learn what Göran Larsson calls "temperance in one's own life." Larsson notes that manna is the food of temperance; it is exactly what a human needs, neither more nor less.[34] We see this in the repeated reference to having only enough manna to provide in each person's need (vv. 8, 12, 16, 18, 21). This is confirmed by the miracle of equality; everybody had just enough to eat and they lacked nothing (v. 18). In this regard, Rolf Knierim's point in reference to the Lord's Prayer is valuable. Knierim argues that the "'daily bread' means that which we *need* from day to day to day, and not more, certainly not the surplus destined for the trash can or the garbage disposal."[35]

Third, Israel had to learn to have just enough to live comfortably, which Larsson calls "solidarity with one's neighbor."[36] Israel had to make sure that all were provided for, sharing the available resources. This third lesson calls to mind the previous dimension of the God who acts as household manager and who fairly measures out food to everybody. One finds in this narrative something of an ethical perspective that calls on Israel to feed the hungry. Knierim raises a similar point with regard to the Lord's Prayer when he asks why the emphasis on daily food has not impelled Christianity to develop a doctrine of food supply for all people? And if such a doctrine were to become commonplace, he wonders, "would [we] exist in a world in which forty thousand infants alone die each day of illness and malnutrition"?[37]

We see from these comments how this understanding of the God who feeds makes an important claim on future generations to live differently, making the lessons of daily trust in God, of temperance in our own lives, and of solidarity with our neighbors our own. This claim is based on the assumption that the portrayal of God within this narrative has and should have an effect on human behavior.[38]

If we use the metaphor of a mother nursing her child to describe Israel's absolute reliance on God, then we could argue that Israel had to learn to trust their mother that tomorrow there would be enough food. It is by the daily experience of God's goodness that this mother slowly instills trust in her children that she will not abandon them. Second, a mother knows how much her child needs to eat, providing just enough to sustain a healthy baby. A mother knows that too little food is harmful to the health of her child, as is too much. This lesson is conveyed to the child, teaching him or her how much to eat. And third, we have seen that God might be portrayed as a mother who fairly measures out food to everybody and teaches her children to do the same.

A Metaphor that Moves People

Thus far, we have seen convincing support for conceiving the metaphor of God's provision of food in female terms. The power of this metaphor to grasp people's imagination is further evident from the rich interpretation history of this metaphor. A number of rabbinic interpreters engaged in some imaginative interpretations employing nursing imagery to describe God's provision of food. But also within the Christian tradition, a metaphor of God nursing became an ingenious way of expressing something of the interpreters' experience of God. For instance, two second-century Christian interpreters employed a nursing image to describe God but developed this metaphor in a distinct fashion when they used this image in conjunction with christological, or in the case of the second text, trinitarian language. The church father Clement of Alexandria gave the following interpretation, in which a life of learning is depicted in terms of the metaphor of nursing: "To Christ the fulfilling of His Father's will was food; and to us infants, who milk the Word of the heavens, Christ Himself is food. Hence seeking is called sucking; for to those infants who seek the Word, the Father's nipples of the love of humankind supply milk."[39]

Another text, *Odes of Sol* 19:1-5, is part of a collection of Christian hymns that have survived in the Syriac language. According to Susan Harvey, traditions of the Eucharist and possibly Baptism may underlie this interpretation, since second-century baptismal rites included the presentation of a cup of milk and honey in addition to the bread and wine to the newly baptized.[40]

> A cup of milk was offered to me,
> and I drank it in the sweetness of the Lord's kindness.
> The Son is the cup,
> and the Father is he who was milked;
> and the Holy Spirit is she who milked him;
> Because his breasts were full,
> and it was undesirable that his milk should be released
> without purpose.
> The Holy Spirit opened her bosom,
> and mixed the milk of the two breasts of the Father.
> Then she gave the mixture to the generation without
> their knowing,
> and those who have received (it) are in the perfection
> of the right hand.[41]

These two examples are indicative of the fact that the metaphor of nursing has become a powerful way of describing God's provision of food and particularly a life of learning. There are many more interpretations that engage in similar theological reflection. For instance, in the Middle Ages, the metaphor of God and Christ nursing is an important symbol and is used by theologians such as Julian of Norwich, Catherine of Siena, and Hildegard of Bingen to describe their theological experience.[42]

Additionally, the connection with the sacraments of the Eucharist and the Baptism add even more to the power of the metaphor as word is enforced by action. In this regard, Ivan Marcus has described the intriguing phenomenon of "the ritualization of metaphors." He shows how a number of medieval Jewish childhood rituals associated with the education of children have ritualized the metaphor of the Torah as bread, oil, milk and honey, and the metaphor of nursing as a symbol of learning that is featured in this chapter. He describes, for instance, how at the commencement of a teaching session, a child is placed on the lap of the teacher who, like Moses, is compared to a nursing mother (Num 11:12). This act grows out of an understanding of the relationship between a small child and teacher in terms of the biblical image of Israel as child and Moses and God as nurturing parent (Num 11:12). In order to teach children the benefit of education, the teacher gives the child "Torah cakes," which are made with oil, flour, milk, and honey—all traditionally equated with the Torah. This custom, which according to Marcus ritualizes the metaphor, has the function of opening up the child's heart to the process of learning. From these associations "a maternal vocabulary emerges that presents Moses, the rabbis, and Torah teachers as nursing mothers who feed their students with Torah."[43]

Something of this "ritualization of the metaphor" is also to be found in the Christian tradition. More will be said about the sacramental nature of the metaphor of God's provision of food in the concluding chapter when some perspectives concerning the Eucharist will be introduced.

From these few excerpts from both Christian and Jewish interpreters, we see evidence of readers being moved by this powerful metaphor, even resulting in rituals that further testify to the power of the metaphor. These interpretations also serve as inspiration to develop the female dimension of the metaphor of the God who feeds. In light of this fascinating interpretation history, we could argue that the metaphor of God as the Mother who feeds her children is genuinely creative and serves the function of creating a new understanding concerning God's provision for her children. A metaphor is not just redescribing but disclosing truth for the first time. The metaphor of God as the Mother who feeds can thus be described as a living metaphor. The reason for this is that there is a dissonance or tension at the heart of this metaphor, as the metaphor tends to cross traditional boundaries.[44] Some people may be shocked by this metaphor, as they are not used to thinking about God in this way. This may exactly be where the power of this metaphor lies. People quite conceivably may listen afresh to the old stories in which the metaphor occurs, thereby moving them toward a new understanding concerning God and their relationship with God.

CHAPTER 2

FEEDING ALL OF CREATION

T hus far, we have seen how God's provision of food offers a striking illustration of God's relationship with Israel. The personal nature of this relationship is illustrated well by the nursing imagery that is employed to describe God's relationship with God's people. However, if one looks elsewhere in the Old Testament, one soon notices that God's care extends beyond the provision of food for the children of Israel to all of creation. God is not only the God of Israel but also of all creatures great and small. This claim has the profound effect of extending a cosmic dimension to God's provision of food—something that has significant implications for our understanding of God as well as our own relationship to the world. In this chapter, I will show how various texts such as Gen 1–2, Job 38, and Pss 104, 145–47 develop this dimension of the metaphor of the God who feeds and in the process add some significant perspectives to our understanding of this metaphor.

SETTING THE TABLE FOR ALL CREATION

God's provision of food to all of creation first manifests itself in the first chapter of the Old Testament when God provides food for the newly created beings. God pronounces in Gen 1:29: "See, I have given you every plant yielding seed that is upon the face of all the earth, and every tree with seed in its fruit; you shall have them for food."

But even before God provides food in verse 29, God has already made provision for this food. In Gen 1:11, the third act of creation is to "let the earth put forth vegetation: plants yielding seed, and fruit trees of every kind." Before God creates the humans and animals, God builds a home for them by forming the earth on which all living creatures will dwell, after which God creates the vegetation necessary for nourishment. One could say that God is setting a food-filled table for all living things by creating the plants and trees that will make life possible.

Also in the Gen 2 creation story, God is portrayed as the God who feeds. The first thing God does after breathing the breath of life into the nostrils of the first human is to plant a garden, full of every kind of tree "that is pleasant to the sight and good for food" (Gen 2:8-9). God places the human in this garden with the function of providing nourishment for the created beings. Once again, before God provides food, God makes provision for this food. Even before it started to rain on the earth (water of course being a necessary precondition for vegetation), God causes a stream to rise from the earth that waters "the whole face of the ground" (Gen 2:5-6).

A similar interpretation is seen in Ps 104. Once more God builds a house for all creatures to live in. God's creative activity of setting the earth on its foundations has the distinct purpose of creating a home out of the primeval waters to sustain creatures through watering, feeding, and dwelling. Within this habitat, God again provides food for all the living beings. In verse 14, God causes "the grass to grow for the cattle, / and plants for people to use, / [and brings] forth food from the earth." The whole psalm builds up to the climactic statement in verses 27-28 where a summary statement is given, which conveys something of the total dependence of all of creation on God:

> *All* of them look to you,
> to give them their food in its season.
> When you give to them, they gather up;
> when you open your hand, they are satisfied with
> good things. (AT)

The sufficiency of God's provision is expressed in three ways. First, it is significant that the writer uses Hebrew verbs in the imperfect tense, thereby denoting action that is incomplete, ongoing, and repetitive. (Cf. the English translation's use of the present tense to convey this meaning.) Second, the phrase that God gives food to all in its proper time, or as the NRSV states "in due season," denotes something of the timely nature of God's provision. God knows what creatures need at which time. Third, this notion is further articulated by the image of God's open hand, which yields "good things" with which the creatures are satisfied. This latter term (שָׂבַע) is also used in relation to God's provision of manna to Israel—manna that was always there and always enough (Exod 16:8, 12). Consequently, the whole world continually depends for its existence on God.

Once more, before God provides food, God makes arrangements for this food. So, in Ps 104:10-13, God dispenses the rain that makes the earth fruitful. From the heavenly storeroom, the earth is satisfied with rain and springs that are allowed to gush forth. This provides the water that is necessary for all living to quench their thirst, as well as the vegetation that supplies food to humans and animals alike.

THE NATURE OF GOD'S PROVISION

These texts clearly disclose something of the continuity between creation and providence, between giving life to the creatures and providing for their existence. An integral part of God's creation is that God provides food to the newly created living beings. God's provision of food exhibits the following characteristics: First, this portrayal reveals something of the *intimate nature* of God's relationship with creation. God is personally involved in the life process of what is created. This is evident in the way God directly addresses the newly created beings, in which God offers blessing and vocation to the humans (Gen 1:28; cf. 1:22), as well as food to satisfy their needs (1:29).[1]

Second, there is an integral connection between *God's gift of life and God's gift of food*. Both creation stories develop this theme. In Gen 1:30, God presents the plant-bearing earth on the sixth day to all the living things, which includes the land animals and the human beings. In order for life to continue, the living beings need food to sustain them. Also in Gen 2:7, God is said to give life when God breathes into the human's nostrils the breath that gives life. This is followed by God's provision of food when God plants the garden with trees that are good for food (Gen 2:8-9). God's gift of life implies that the newly created being also receives the means to live.

This idea is also conveyed in Ps 104:28-29 where God's provision of food is once more connected with life. Immediately after the claim that God provides food to all who breathe the breath of life, the poet admits that when God takes away their breath, they die and return to the dust from which they came. This integral connection between life and food is

25

significant as it points to the fact that the God who has given life does everything possible to sustain this life.

Third, there is an *aesthetic quality* to God's provision of food. This echoes something of what Walter Brueggemann calls the "aesthetic dimension" of creation, "that exults in the artistry of God, in the beauty of the created order."[2] In Gen 1, the refrain "God saw that it was good" is repeatedly used to describe the newly fashioned creation (vv. 4, 10, 12, 18, 21, 25, 31). God's creation, in which food plays a significant role, is good. Moreover, Gen 2:9 explicitly says that the food that God provides for human consumption has not only a functional element to it but also an aesthetic dimension in that God makes every tree that is pleasant to the sight and good for food.

Also in Ps 104, God's gift of food extends beyond mere utilitarian value and expresses something of the generosity of God's gift. In verse 15 God's gift of food not only includes the daily bread to strengthen the human heart but also wine to gladden the heart and oil to make the face shine. God's gifts of abundance are there to bring joy to people, to make them strong, happy, and beautiful.[3] God's gifts of food reach the inner being—something that becomes visible in the face that shines with oil. In Patrick Miller's words: "The goal of creation, in its details and in its whole, is to provide pleasure and delight."[4]

Fourth, another important point to consider concerning God's provision of food is that God is providing food to *all* creation. Genesis 1:29-30 clearly states that food is given not only to humans but also to every beast of the earth, the birds of the air, and everything creeping on the face of the earth. God provides for humans every plant that bears seed and every tree with seed in its fruit as food and for the animals green plants. This close relation between humans and animals is evident from the fact that both humans and animals are described as having the breath of life (נפש חיה in Gen 1:30 and 2:7). Moreover, both humans and animals receive the same blessing. Genesis 1 portrays human beings as sharing their earthly home and its resources with the other land creatures that were created on the sixth day, thereby creating a sense of the interconnectedness of all life instead of asserting the superiority of humankind. In addition, the fact that the first page of the Bible makes such a strong point of including the birds, fish, and animals in God's provision of food is a clear sign that God is concerned with all of them. One could thus say that God's care is all-inclusive, extending to all life.

Also in Ps 104, one finds that God's care extends to all of creation. Once more the cattle are fed right next to the humans. In fact, their provision is even mentioned prior to the exposition of the human's sustenance (vv. 14-15). In addition, verses 21-22 say that the young lions roar for their prey, seeking their food from God. As verse 25 concludes, living things both small and great, the ships with all on board, and even the Leviathan, that strange, dangerous, scary monster that embodied all that Israel feared, look to God to give them food in due season, to fill them with good things. Psalm 104 thus portrays the human species as simply one more of God's creatures, who, along with the cattle and other animals, are dependent on God's provision of sustenance. In what James Mays calls "the poetic portrait of the world," as portrayed in verses 10-23, "all are interrelated in the great web of the works of the Lord."[5]

In Job 38, God's provision of food extends once more to the animal kingdom. Verses 39-40 ask the rhetorical question of whether Job can hunt the lion's prey or provide sufficiently for the young lions. The answer to this rhetorical question is of course a firm no. Moreover, verse 41 inquires as to the identity of the one who feeds the raven, when the young ravens cry in their hunger to God. Again the expected answer is that it is not Job who is fulfilling this function, but God. The lion and raven form part of a list of animals in Job 38–39, including the "ibex, hind, wild donkey, bullock, ostrich, horse, peregrine falcon, and vulture"—all of whom share in God's special care.[6] These animals have in common that they are associated with places outside of and opposed to the human cultural sphere.[7] Carol Newsom argues that God uses the wild animals to confront Job with something that will not fit his previously held categories of "mastery and dependence," which were inevitably drawn from Job's "social world of village patriarchy." The animals signify a dimension of creation that stands outside "the domination and utility of humans," thereby symbolizing "the excluded and alienated others" that are to be understood in terms of "nondependence and nondomination."[8]

Psalm 147 yields another glimpse of God's provision that extends to all creation. In verse 9 God gives the animals their food. This claim is specified by the reference, "to the young ravens when they cry." This statement is to be understood in light of the following verse, where God does not take pleasure in the strength on which human beings rely, as is represented by the "strength of the horse" or the "speed of a runner." The young ravens, whose cries are heard as a prayer to which God gives answer, therefore become a model of the utter reliance of all of creation upon God's gracious provision.[9]

The church fathers and medieval interpreters understood the young ravens to be the faithful who pray to God (this in contrast to the older ravens who signify the heathen or unrepentant sinners).[10] Such an interpretation instills in its readers' imaginations the realization that humans are completely dependent on God's power to support and maintain the world and all its inhabitants. Verse 11 praises those individuals who grasp their reliance on God and who are constantly hoping in God's gracious faithfulness and love.

This interpretation is also very much at the heart of the New Testament interpretation of Luke 12:24 where God *feeds* the ravens (ὁ θεὸς τρέφει), which do not sow or reap, nor have storehouses or barns (all activities that humans participate in to secure food). Thus, God cares for the ravens, which, contrary to people, do nothing to secure their basic needs of sustenance. Using the power of imagination, this image from nature has the effect of inviting the audience to look at the world in a new way. They are reminded of God's gracious provision of food to all of creation, and in the process, they are encouraged to notice the God who cares for them.[11]

A question remains, however. If God is the One who feeds all creatures big and small, what role do humans or animals play in this provision? Are the creatures only passive objects, or do they engage in some kind of activity to make God's provision of food a reality? One sees this problem well illustrated in Ps 104:14-15. Is it God who provides food? Or is it the human whose work in the fields provides the wine, oil, and bread? It seems as if there is something of a double agency at work; thus, God provides food by means of human hands. In Ps 104, bread does not fall from heaven; food is generally derived from human labor. Nevertheless, it still is God's gift that enables the labor and God's rain that ensures a productive harvest.

One sees a further connection between God's work and the creaturely work in Ps 104:21-23, where the daily rhythms of work and rest to which animals and humans alike adhere are mentioned. The young lions that hunt at night, roaring for their prey, know to rest with daybreak—daybreak being the time when humans go out to work and labor until the evening. Thus, although Ps 104 makes the claim that all creatures look to God to give their food at its appropriate time, God's gift of sustenance implies daily work.[12]

A Broken World

Despite the powerful evidence that God is the benevolent creator, who not only gives life to all living things but also sustains God's creatures by providing the sustenance necessary for life to continue, one cannot escape the fact that the reality of life around us is a constant reminder that this is not the whole story. If one says that God's bounty extends to all, how is it possible that people are dying of hunger? The Food and Agriculture Organization of the United Nations estimates that 841 million people are currently suffering from inadequate access to food.[13] If we say that God's provision of food is a loving, beneficent gift, why do so many people, and especially children, suffer from obesity and other eating disorders?[14] The reality of life is that we are living in a broken world, full of hurt and pain.

The seed of this suffering is already found in the structure of the first story in the Old Testament. Yes, Gen 1–3 provides a wonderful view of God providing food to all. However, the irony is that within this gift of food, the potential for destruction is already present. The same food that was said in Gen 2:9 to be "pleasant to the sight and good for food" contained the potential to become a vehicle of death.

But how did this happen? The reason for this sad situation is to be found in human disobedience to God's command. In Gen 2, God provides food of great abundance and freedom: the humans can freely eat of all the trees in the garden. Except for one restriction. In the midst of God's provision of food, God includes a command: the humans can fully enjoy God's abundant gifts, except for one tree that is off limits, the tree of the knowledge of good and evil. This tree carries the threat of death. Whereas the fruit of all the other trees will bring life to its partakers, this one tree will bring death.

When the serpent plays on the humans' natural inclination to be curious, informing the woman that they will not die but that eating from the tree will make them "like God, knowing good and evil" (v. 5), the woman notices in verse 6 that the tree was indeed good for food and beautiful to look at. This is similar to language that was used earlier to describe all the other trees by means of which God provides food ("pleasant to the sight and good for food," v. 9). However, there is an added phrase in verse 6, which states that eating from this tree will make one wise.[15] And eating from this tree would go straight against God's commandment. As Phyllis Trible notes,

To eat and not to eat: permission and prohibition unite in a double command that is designed to preserve life. This command points up the opposites that can result from a single act. To eat is to live: "from every tree ... you may surely eat," for the trees are "pleasant to see and good to eat." Yet to eat is to die: "for when you eat of it [the tree of the knowledge of good and evil] you will surely die." One act, eating, holds both life and death. The difference lies in obeying or disobeying the limits set by God.[16]

But the woman eats, and her husband eats too.[17] In Gen 3:11, God describes their disobedience as follows: "Have you eaten from the tree of which I commanded you not to eat?" By eating from the forbidden fruit, the human beings rebelled against their Creator, yielding to the temptation to "be like God" (Gen 3:5, 22). The consequence of this act is that the human beings upset their relationship with God and accordingly their relationship with each other and with the earth, to which they are closely related and on which they depend for their existence.

Within the ensuing punishment, it is important to note that human disobedience impacts God's provision of food. Because of their sin, the ground is cursed. This has implications for God's continuing provision of food. Whereas the human beings, before the fall, could freely eat from all the trees in the garden that were just ready for the picking, in the punishment, the food is now accompanied with pain and hardship. There will be "thorns and thistles," and the provision of bread will be accompanied by hard, toilsome labor. As verse 19 notes: "by the sweat of your face / you shall eat bread." Because of their disobedience, the earth that brings forth food for the human beings to eat is contaminated, as is the food of God's provision.

We see something of this in the continuing reality of a broken world today. The consequences of human disobedience endure in the persisting problem of injustice in the world. There are some who go without food because of the disobedience of others. There are only a limited amount of resources in the world, so if some people take more than their share, there is less to go around. This broken reality is also present when human society's fascination with the perfect body leads to eating disorders. Or when people try to fill some void in their life with food. Then food, which is supposed to be a good thing—nourishing the body and bringing joy to the soul—is permeated with complexity.[18]

However, despite the desperate situation our broken world presents, all is not lost. One sees evidence of this when God's provision of food does not stop. Even while God is punishing the humans in Gen 3, God is still providing food: "You shall eat the plants of the field" (v. 18). Even in the midst of punishment, God's care continues. This is also seen in God's caring act in Gen 3:20 (21 MT), when God makes garments of skin for the humans and clothes them. God is like the parent who, even though he or she is furious with the child's disobedience, continues to remember the child's needs.

One also finds in Job 38 that God's provision of food is acutely linked to the broken world in which evil and chaos form an undeniable part. God does not annihilate the chaos and brokenness in the world but confines it within certain boundaries, just as God restricted the Leviathan and Behemoth. Job 38:8-11 speaks about the confinement of the chaos waters. According to Norman Habel, the control of the sea as primordial chaos monster is likened to the tending of a baby. He suggests that "the image is deliberately absurd. The violent chaos monster is but an infant, born from a womb, wrapped in baby clothes, placed in a playpen, and told to stay in its place."[19]

The continuing presence of chaos and evil also influences God's provision of food. Consequently, God's provision of food does not make for a romantic picture. In Job 38:39-41, God hunts on behalf of the lions and kills prey to satisfy their appetite. But if one thinks about it, Habel is right when he says that "the food for the lion and the kill for the raven are innocent creatures who no more deserve to die than any others." The broken world in which God's provision of food occurs implies that "the baby eagle survives because another young creature dies."[20] As Habel so aptly describes this fact, "God does not eliminate the forces of chaos, the role of Death, or the presence of the wicked. They operate within the eternal constraints of the design. Life is balanced by darkness."[21]

For this reason, it is crucial to realize that the world we live in is paradoxical in its very design and permeated by incongruities. It is a world where the regular and the unpredicted, the good and the evil, the hunter and the prey coexist. Thus, even something as beneficial as God's gracious provision of food is not void of complexity.

Also in Ps 104 there is a note of dissonance. In verse 29, a reference is made to what happens when God hides God's face. In the midst of the ode to God's wondrous provision for all creation, God hides God's face. The same creatures that were just satisfied with all good things are now dismayed. God, the giver of life, also gives death when God takes away the breath of life so that the "all" that was mentioned in verse 27 returns to the dust from which they came. Psalm 104 is admitting that life is not perfect and that, although nature is good and valuable, there is a shadow side to God's creation.[22]

Nevertheless, despite the acceptance of this undeniable reality, Ps 104 also submits that the chaotic waters of the primeval ocean have lost their destructive potency. Psalm 104:9 states that God set a boundary that the water is not allowed to cross. The once threatening water of chaos is transformed to form a life-giving fountain that offers the necessary water to sustain all creation. It is as if Ps 104 wants to suggest that although evil and chaos are part of the world, God does not annihilate the chaos but is able to hold the chaos at bay.

JUSTICE AND DIVINE FEEDING

In the previous section, we read how human disobedience permeates God's provision of food. The consequence of this broken reality is that there are some who have too much, and as a result, others go to bed hungry. However, if we make the claim that God provides food to all, it means exactly that: God makes sure that *all* God's children have enough to eat—especially those who are not able to fend for themselves. Thus, an integral part of God's provision of food is justice and righteousness for those who are oppressed and poor. Something of this perspective is found in the rabbinic interpretation on Ps 104:17. (Italics represent a quotation within a quotation.) "*That Thou givest them, they gather* (Ps. 104:28): Out of what He gives to the rich, the Holy One, blessed be He, sustains the poor. In *Thou openest thy hand, they are filled with good* (ibid.), *they* is meant to include poor and rich alike."[23]

This is further illustrated in Ps 145:14 where God is called the God of the downtrodden, who raises up those who are bowed down. This claim is immediately followed by the statement that the eyes of *all* look to God, who gives them their food at the right time (v. 15; see also Ps 104:27). God's provision of food is all-sufficient, satisfying the desire of all living things (v. 16). The constancy of God's provision of food is underlined by the repeated use of participles employed in this depiction of God (נותן; פותח; ומשׁביע). This notion is consistently present in the portrayal of God's provision of food thus far. However in Pss 145–47, we encounter an additional perspective when a connection is made between God's provision of food and the belief that God executes justice for the oppressed.

32

Indeed God's provision of food extends to *all* people, especially those who are hungry.

In Norbert Lohfink's interpretation of Ps 147:9, he argues that the young raven is a reference to the poor, continuing the theme of God caring for the helpless and the "little" people. Lohfink bases this interpretation, among other things, on the fact that the word that is used to describe the raven's cry (יקראו) is the same word that is used to describe the cries of the poor in Deut 15:9 and 24:15.[24] The theme that God cares for those who have little power and live in total trust of God is a leading theme that echoes throughout the Psalms. For instance, in Ps 146:7-8, God executes justice for the oppressed, gives food to the hungry, sets the prisoners free, opens the eyes of the blind, lifts up those who are bowed down, and loves the righteous. Once more a connection is made between God's justice and God's provision of food. It is very much a part of God's identity to care for everyone, particularly those on the margins.

These psalms reiterate the biblical claim that God is in a special way the God of the poor and the oppressed, the widow, orphan, and foreigner. As Deut 10:18 says: "[God] executes justice for the orphan and the widow, and...loves the strangers, providing them food and clothing." This understanding finds its way into the New Testament when Luke 1:53 states that God fills the hungry with good things, right after it is said that God raises up the lowly and brings down the powerful from their thrones.

However, these psalms make another important claim. They admit that life is not perfect. They acknowledge the broken reality of people who are poor and hungry and do not overlook those people whom society has relegated to the margins—in biblical times, the widow, the orphan, the foreigner, and the poor. As Brueggemann notes, "The very mention of them is an act of social realism and social criticism. Marginal people really do exist."[25] This acknowledgment should serve as encouragement for us never to forget the broken reality in which we live or to overlook the imperfections of life. The portrayal of God as One who notices and intervenes on behalf of those who dwell on the margins of society and who are not able to fend for themselves should challenge us to do something to make things right, to follow God's example in pursuing justice and feeding the hungry.

But although these psalms speak truthfully about the broken reality and notice those that are ordinarily overlooked, the psalms still tend to lack particulars. For instance, in reference to Ps 145, Brueggemann notes that "the praises of Israel have been generalized and move to description."

These claims, which are expressed in participles, denote not specificity but generality, not concrete expressions but stereotyped perceptions. Although the psalm makes powerful and sweeping claims, "it lacks all specificity, every reference to a time, a place, and identifiable subject."[26]

In this regard, Frank Fromherz's comment regarding the significance of particular stories in the quest for restoring the right relationship with God, each other, and all of creation is important. He says:

> How can one possibly respond to a call to live in right relationship with *all* of creation or *every* human being? Justice is better understood not as a rigid and abstract principle, like a giant anvil dropped into the flower garden of our fragile lives, but rather as a call heard sometimes faintly and now and then poignantly as real stories are shared and collective narratives of sin and grace are encountered. Justice, in this view, is intrinsically relational and invites a turn to stories in order that we may recognize creaturely relations with particular creation—not "all of creation" in the abstract.[27]

The fact that the poor, widows, orphans, and hungry all remain faceless and void of specificity is illustrated well by an interpretation from the midrash on the Psalms. The rabbinic interpreters noticed this problem in their question on Ps 146:7. (Italics represent a quotation within a quotation.) They asked, "Who is meant by *the hungry?*" when it says in Ps 146:7, *"[God] who executeth justice for the oppressed; who giveth bread to the hungry."* According to the rabbis, the answer is Elijah. For "he was hungry, and God gave him bread to eat, as is said [in 1 Kgs 17:6], *And the ravens brought him bread and flesh in the morning, and bread and flesh in the evening; and he drank of the brook*" (Ps 146:4).[28]

The case of Elijah is indeed an instance of God providing for the hungry. However, there are other stories in which the claim that God feeds the hungry and takes special care of the poor, the widow, the orphan, and the stranger becomes very real. For instance, in the book of Ruth, the disenfranchised receives a face: Ruth, the foreigner who comes from Moab with her mother-in-law, the widow who was left to fend for herself after her husband's death. Ruth and her mother-in-law can rightly be described as being poor and hungry. The repeated designation, "Ruth, the Moabite" that is to be found throughout the book (see, e.g., Ruth 1:22; 2:2, 21; 4:5, 10), emphasizes Ruth's status as a foreigner in particular. In Ruth 1:6, we encounter the claim once again that God feeds the hungry. We read that Naomi has heard that God has considered God's people and given them food. This comment evokes once more the image of God as provider of sustenance for all creation. Although this claim is talking about God's care for Israel, the leading theme of the book of Ruth is how a foreigner shares in this gift. Ruth's story becomes a concrete illustration of how God feeds the hungry, the widow, and the stranger.

God's provision of food is executed in two ways in the book of Ruth. First, as a "poor non-Israelite woman," Ruth depends on the means of survival as provided for in Israelite law.[29] According to the custom of that time, the have-nots from society were allowed to go gleaning, that is, after the harvest, they could go pick up ears of corn and wheat that were left over. Deuteronomy 24:19-22 gives the following command:

> When you reap your harvest in your field and forget a sheaf in the field, you shall not go back to get it; it shall be left for the alien, the orphan, and the widow, so that the LORD your God may bless you in all your undertakings. When you beat your olive trees, do not strip what is left; it shall be for the alien, the orphan, and the widow. When you gather the grapes of your vineyard, do not glean what is left; it shall be for the alien, the orphan, and the widow. Remember that you were a slave in the land of Egypt; therefore I am commanding you to do this.

Thus, by means of the gleaning laws God's provision of food is made real. Although times change and concepts like gleaning fall strange on one's modern ear, the phenomenon of the marginalized people struggling for survival is timeless. Katharine Doob Sakenfeld actualizes these gleaning laws. "Gleaning continues in various forms in the modern world as a means of survival for the destitute. In some countries, it is structured by law, routinized as a welfare safety net, or organized through food banks; but even there, people rummage through garbage cans to survive. In some poorer nations, conditions for the destitute in search of food are even more extreme."[30]

This modern day example raises poignant questions about the fate of the poor and hungry in our own societies, particularly by what means God's provision of food could be realized today.

Second, God's provision of food to the poor, the hungry, the widow, and the foreigner is realized through the kindness of one man. Called a man of valor, Boaz becomes an instrument in God's hands to provide for the stranger and the widow. This is clearly seen in Ruth 2:14 and 18, where Boaz provides Ruth with food in abundance. He gave her more than she could eat, and after she had eaten her fill, she took what was left over home to feed another hungry widow, her mother-in-law, Naomi.

Boaz's actions go beyond what was expected. Not only does he provide Ruth with food, but his invitation to her to sit with the other workers functions as a gesture of inclusion into the larger community.[31] Although God's gift of food is a strong presence in the Old Testament, the story of Ruth indicates that human action is required in the full realization of this gift. As Sakenfeld notes, "Divine provision of potential sustenance is a necessary beginning point, but only a beginning."[32] Accordingly, readers are encouraged to look for ways in which God's blessings can be realized through their actions toward others.

Finally, the story of Ruth provides ample evidence to counter the tendency that still exists to claim God's provision only for oneself. Something of this tendency is evident in the rabbinic interpretation of Ps 146:6, where "those who are bowed down" in Ps 146:8 is equated with Israel. (Italics represent a quotation within a quotation.) *"The Lord raises up them that are bowed down (Ps 146:8): Who are bowed down?* The children of Israel who are exiled from the Land of Israel. Ever since the day that they were exiled from Jerusalem, they have not been able to stand up straight, but are bowed down so low before their enemies that their enemies walk all over them."[33]

Although this is surely an acceptable interpretation, the portrait of God's provision of food extending to all creation provides strong evidence that the claim in a psalm like Ps 146 could and should be extended to cross boundaries of race, gender, and socioeconomic standing.

A METAPHOR WITH TRANSFORMING POWER

Thus far, we have encountered some powerful connotations raised by the metaphor of the God who feeds all of creation. An ensuing question is, what rhetorical effect does this metaphor have for our understanding of God and our relationship with the world in which we dwell? Newsom has argued that the divine speeches in Job present Job with "an alternative set of radical metaphors, formal patterns, and modes of perception capable of generating a fundamentally different moral imagination than that by which Job had previously lived."[34] I propose that the metaphor of God's provision of food to all creation has a similar effect, providing an "alternative moral vision" that may affect the way an individual experiences God and views his or her place in the world.

First, it is important to note that the metaphor of the God who feeds all creation necessitates response. The glorious portrayal of creation in Ps 104:10-23 is followed by the spontaneous exclamation in verse 24: "O LORD, how manifold are your works! In wisdom you have made them all; the earth is full of your creatures." The psalm culminates in a praise song dedicated to the Creator God (vv. 31-35). It seems as if the chief purpose of the description of the creaturely dependence of life upon the Creator is that the hearer shall revel in the wonder of it all.

The same thing is true of the creation story in Gen 1. With repetitive frequency, the refrain, "God saw that it was good," follows each one of God's creative acts. And after God's provision of sustenance to the newly created beings, God responds with satisfaction, "Indeed, it was very good." God's creation, and in particular God's provision of food to all creation, most certainly calls for appreciation and praise.[35]

Similarly in Ps 145, there is a distinct link between praise and God's provision of food. The claim of God as the ultimate provider of food does not stand alone but rather in the context of the previous call to praise in verses 1-12. Once more, one cannot stand unresponsive to God's provision of food to all creation.

Second, the knowledge that God is the God who feeds all creation may have a profound effect on how we live our lives. To know that God is the God who feeds all creation may once again instill in us the realization that we are completely dependent on God for all of our needs. This portrayal of God encourages us to look up from our own complicated lives, to look out the window, to put things in perspective. One could say that if God is the One who feeds the entire cosmos, surely God will be able to take care of me as well. According to Siegfried Risse, the church fathers (e.g., the fourth-century interpreter John Chrysostom) interpreted God's provision for the young ravens in Ps 147:9 in precisely this fashion. This interpretation is also picked up in the New Testament, when Luke 12:24 says, "Consider the ravens: they neither sow nor reap, they have neither storehouse nor barn, and yet God feeds them." Luke 12 makes the claim that if God is feeding God's other creatures, will God not feed you much more? (See also Matt 6:33.)[36]

However, it is true that one cannot make this claim without thinking of the millions of people who are leading a life characterized by starvation or considering the thousands of people for whom food has become a curse. A text like Luke 12:22-34 challenges its audience to a new understanding of God's character and purpose. To really *know* God as the

caring provider will enable people to reorient their lives and live according to God's will. Joel Green says, "If they could accept his portrait of the
caring God who provides for them, as the Father whose pleasure is manifest in his provision of the kingdom, would this not be impetus enough
for a radically reconstructed attitude toward and set of behaviors concerning 'the abundance of possessions'?"[37]

Such an interpretation encourages the reader to focus not merely on
his or her own needs but also to keep the needs of others in mind.
Newsom proposes that God directs Job away from his primary horizon of
the family and the village, where "mastery and dependence" was the only
governing principle, to the cosmos itself—a cosmos where there are
beings that can rightly be considered to be genuine "others." These "others" cannot be controlled in the way to which Job had been accustomed.
Accordingly, a third implication of the metaphor of the God who feeds
all creation is that it encourages us to realize that God has other creatures
as well. We are often so busy with our own lives that we tend to forget
this important claim. God's provision of food is crucial to understand that
God not only provides food to my family and me but also to the rest of
the world community. What is more, God is even feeding the Leviathan,
the strangest of the strange, that "thing" that everyone feared. To understand this has implications for how we perceive people in our own society who tend to be overlooked, feared, judged, and looked down upon.
God is also their God. God is also feeding the outsider. As Newsom suggests, Job's encounter with God caused him to look on society's outcasts
with different eyes. Job's seeing was altered.[38]

The metaphor of God's provision of food in the story of Ruth and Pss
145–47 has a similar effect. These texts serve as a powerful reminder that
God is a God of justice. Moreover, the story of Ruth reminds us of the
value of putting faces on the abstract categories of the marginalized. We
love to talk about those groups of people: the poor, those who find themselves on welfare, the illiterate. But in the rabbinic interpreters' words:
"Who are they?" Ruth's story encourages us to remember the stories, the
names, and the faces of our brothers and sisters who are poor and hungry.
It challenges us to put faces on those "foreigners" whom we so easily put
into some category, regardless of their rich diversity. The God who feeds
is indeed a God who executes justice for the foreigner, the widow, the
orphan, and the poor.

Fourth, to think of the God who feeds all creation affects how we see
our relationship to the rest of the world. In Gen 1:26 God says: "Let us

create the human in our image [בצלמנו], according to our likeness [כדמותנו]" (AT). The Hebrew word for "image" (צלם) means "statue," thereby saying that human beings are a kind of living image or statue of God. Thus, "to have dominion" (וירדו) over creation implies that humans ought to be representatives of God, signaling God's divine presence.[39] So, as representatives of God, we should represent God in taking care of all creation—in contrast to the traditional interpretation of "to have dominion" (רדה) as "to step on/trample." This view calls the well-known essay by Lynn White to mind. White has argued that Christianity bears a huge burden of guilt for the ecological crisis because Western civilization has created a sharp dichotomy between humankind (history) and its environment (nature). According to White, Christianity "not only established a dualism of man and nature but also insisted that it is God's will that man exploit nature for his proper ends."[40]

As God is feeding all creation, we too are called to this ongoing, continuous act of nurture. We are called to protect the environment, all the animals, big and small, as well as the habitat that is home to all of God's creatures. God works miracles through the efforts of ordinary people, through relief workers dealing with world hunger and agencies dealing with eating disorders. These acts of kindness grow out of compassion, what Wendy Farley describes as "a power that is wounded by the suffering of others and that is propelled into action on their behalf."[41]

Mother to All the Universe

So what does this portrayal of God feeding all creation mean for a feminist interpretation of the metaphor of the God who feeds? We have seen in chapter 1 how there is compelling evidence to imagine the metaphor of the God who feeds in terms of a mother nursing her child. But already in that case, the explicitly female imagery associated with this metaphor was scant to say the least. In the case of gender-neutral texts such as Exod 16 or Deut 8, an extra hermeneutical move was required in order to imagine this metaphor in a female fashion.

This is also true of the texts introduced in this chapter. There is nothing specifically female in the claim that God provides sustenance to all of creation. However, Elizabeth Johnson has suggested something of the potential of this metaphor to be imagined in terms of God as Mother. "Since it is women whose bodies bear, nourish, and deliver new persons into life and, as society is traditionally structured, are most often charged with the responsibility to nurture and raise them into maturity, language about God as Mother carries a unique power to express human relationship to the mystery who generates and cares for everything."[42]

Maternal imagery beautifully expresses the interdependence and interrelatedness of life. The power of this imagery is situated in the fact that all humans, male and female, are born from the bodies of their mothers and are mostly fed by them. Therefore, this imagery expresses the most basic reality of existence.

If one consciously decides to imagine the metaphor of God's provision of food to all creation in this fashion, a feminist construction may look something like this. To imagine the God who feeds all creation in terms of a mother who is intimately involved with her children has the effect of understanding God as caring about the most basic needs of life in our daily struggles. This suggests a mother who has given life to her offspring and who takes the responsibility onto herself to continue the provision of food as long as the child needs it—first from her own body, later by putting nutritious food on the table. Also, God does not just provide for her children's basic necessities, but within this provision there is also an element of joyful abundance. God presents her children with special treats that make her children happy.

Moreover, this Mother's love extends to all of creation. God is the Mother who makes sure that all her children have enough to eat, who is concerned with the well-being of the entire household of the universe. Sallie McFague formulates this cosmocentric perspective: "This God cares about just and sustainable planetary management, so that all creatures may flourish. This God will judge harshly those who do not consider the lilies or who kill a sparrow or who take extra helpings at the table when others are hungry."[43]

Thus, God as Mother is not partial to any of her children. She has a place in her heart for every one of them, even though the children fight among themselves. And the child, whom the other children treat harshly because he or she does not "fit in," holds a special place in her heart. And like any good Mother, God tries to teach the other children to "play nice" with those who are younger or weaker. Moreover, God as Mother always looks for opportunities to show her children that sharing is a valuable virtue to learn.

But as Mother, God's provision of food should not be overly romanticized. Many mothers know the hardships involved in feeding too many mouths with too little resources. This is particularly evident in countries today that experience serious food shortage. Many mothers will go without food to ensure that their families have enough, raising intriguing questions concerning a God who not only suffers with but also suffers on behalf of her children. The claim that God is feeding all of her children admits that we are living in a broken world with lots of pain and suffering to go around. This is something that we will see vividly illustrated in the next chapter when people had to make sense of times of famine, that is, those times when Israel experienced that God fails to feed her children.

WHEN GOD DOES NOT FEED

Perspectives on Famine in the Biblical Traditions

Up to this point, we have discovered the richness of the metaphor of the God who feeds. We have seen how God's care for Israel, as well as for all of creation, is described in terms of food. However, the flip side of this image is when there is famine in the land. Particularly in the prophetic books, one finds vivid descriptions of the suffering people's experience when the food bins run dry. It is then that people may conclude that God sometimes fails to feed God's people.

For instance, in Joel 1, one experiences something of the devastation caused by food scarcity. In verses 4-7 it seems as if the famine was caused by a swarm of locusts, which like a powerful and numerous army invaded the land and devoured everything in sight (v. 6). The piling up of terms in verse 4 evokes, like Bruce Birch suggests, the image of "the piling up of these insect bodies as they swarm across the land eating everything in sight."[1] The effect of this vivid description is one of complete devastation: nothing remains after the locusts sweep by.

On the other hand, Graham Ogden argues that the locust imagery is not a description of an actual locust plague but forms part of a series of metaphors (cf. drought in Joel 1:9-13, 17-18 and fire in Joel 1:19-20; 2:3) that is used to describe an enemy invasion. These metaphors describe the destruction that the powerful enemy has brought about, and particularly the shortage of food that is caused by the enemy's invasion.[2]

Whether locusts mean the destruction of an enemy army or whether it is the other way around cannot be determined for certain. What is true is that a terrible tragedy, the likes of which never had been seen before (vv. 2-3), evoked other images of similarly destructive events. This merger of metaphors shares a common element, that is, that all these devastating events (locusts, fire, drought, and enemy invasion) lead to food scarcity of frightening proportions.

The famine imagery in Joel 1 stands in stark contrast with the previous chapters where God's provision of food for Israel and all of creation was always there and always enough. The most basic provisions for Israel have ceased to exist (v. 10): the grain is destroyed, the newly pressed wine has dried up, and the fresh oil has failed. Verse 7 tells us how the locusts— like an invading army, powerful, without number, and with dangerous fangs like a lion—have destroyed the vines and the fig trees (symbols for the bountiful production of the land). Finally, verse 12 declares how there is no more fruit, how the vine withers, the fig tree languishes, and the pomegranate, palm, and apple trees have dried up. The picture that is created is one of total devastation, instilling a sense of the gravity of the situation.

Within a subsistence economy with no saving accounts to fall back on, no food almost certainly meant starvation for many. But this lack of food didn't just threaten people's survival. In verse 12 the food shortage is accompanied by a lack of joy. As with the vines and the crops, their joy also withered. The effect of this is that there truly is a famine of joy in the community. Moreover, famine has a spiritual dimension as the lack of food adversely affects the people's practice of religion. The inability to bring food offerings to God (v. 13, cf. Lev 23:18) further increases the distance between God and God's people. Famine indeed strikes at many different levels.

And the famine did not only wrench the life out of the humans. In contrast with the previous chapter where God's provision of food was distinctly said to extend also to the animals, the animals join the lament when the cattle groan "because there is no pasture for them; / [and] even the flocks of sheep are dazed" (v. 18). Humans and animals together plead for God's intervention (see also Jonah 3:7-8). In verse 10, the ground also mourns the lack of food, continuing the idea found in chapter 2 where the earth also was affected by the people's sin.

These images form a sharp contrast with the positive images in chapters 1 and 2 of this book, where God's care for Israel and all creation is celebrated. However, as the current chapter will indicate, famine imagery forms an integral part of the biblical prophets' theological imagination.

FAMINE IN THE OLD TESTAMENT

There are two perspectives in the Old Testament as to how to interpret famine. In the first instance, famine was understood as a natural event that constituted one of the great problems humans had to face (e.g., the example of Abraham in Gen 12:10 and Joseph in Gen 37–50). Together with war, pestilence, and earthquakes, famine offered significant challenges to Israel and fell with little discrimination upon both the just and the unjust. In these instances, famine had to be faced by persons and groups. Its effects should be mitigated and, when possible, overcome. Second, particularly the prophets portray famine as a sign of the sin and failure of human beings. In Amos 4:6-12, God sends all kinds of afflictions upon people as a summons for them to repent and return to God. In Amos's theological framework, famine, drought, mildew, blight, and pestilence are natural events that served to urge people to inquire as to the reason for their occurrence and to inquire into ways to remedy the situation.[3]

These two perspectives on famine illustrate the controversy about how to interpret Joel. According to Birch, Joel sees the famine (whether by locusts, drought, or enemy invasion) as the judgment of God and the prophet's message as a call to lamentation and repentance. We see this particularly in Joel 2:12-17 where the people are called to repentance, to turn to God (lit., "turn to me with all your heart" שֻׁבוּ עָדַי בְּכָל־לְבַבְכֶם) with "fasting, weeping, and mourning" (AT).[4] In contrast, Ogden interprets Joel in terms of the Old Testament lament tradition, where people cry for God's deliverance from what the speaker sees as an undeserved calamity (e.g., Pss 17:3-5; 26:1-3; 44:17-22; 59:3-4). He argues that Joel does not condemn Judah for injustice like the other prophets and that the current crisis should not be interpreted as divine judgment. Ogden argues that when Joel says in 2:12, "turn to me with all your heart," this should be interpreted as "turn to God for assistance."[5]

On a basic level, שׁוּב signifies a spatial designation, "turn to" or "return to."[6] If one reads this language in light of the prophetic tradition where

45

שוב is brought into connection with sin and suffering, the שוב language indeed receives the connotation of "repent" as Birch argues. However, Ogden is right that nowhere in Joel is there any mention of Judah's sin (in contrast with Jeremiah, Amos, and Hosea).[7] Thus, if one reads the שוב language in terms of the lament tradition, it does receive a different connotation of turning to God in a time of crisis—without the penitential motif. As we will see in the following sections, thus, I would say that both of these interpretative stances contain valuable perspectives concerning the metaphor of when God does not feed.

FAMINE AS RADICAL SUFFERING: LAMENTING IN THE FACE OF HUNGER—JOEL AND LAMENTATIONS

There are indeed occasions when the only thing one can do in times of famine is lament. Suffering, and particularly "radical suffering," cannot always be traced to punishment. Wendy Farley argues that "we live in a world where little girls are raped and beaten by their fathers and where war ravages the most helpless and wretched of the earth's children."[8] And in reference to world famine, the tragic reality today is that millions of people starve daily for no reason at all. In situations such as these, it seems as if there is no other option but to sing our laments and to utterly depend on God for deliverance.

In light of this, Joel urges the people to turn to the One who in the past provided food. Joel calls on the people to sing laments, to express their grief publicly, and to engage in rituals of fasting and wearing sackcloth (Joel 1:5-14). In verse 8, Joel urges the people to lament with the same intensity as a young girl whose fiancé has died right before their wedding. Also in Joel 2:13, Ogden interprets the statement, "rend your hearts and not your garments," as a call for deep inner response. Ogden does not see this language as pointing to a call for repentance but rather as indicating heartfelt lament about the current crisis.[9]

Another instance where lament is considered to be the only feasible option is in the book of Lamentations, which contains the cries of Jerusalem's inhabitants after the city was destroyed. Lamentations provides us with some graphic descriptions of the tragedy of war, of the horrors when one's city and home are destroyed, and of the suffering that is associated with the ravages of famine.

In Lamentations, the poetic device of personification is used to convey this experience of suffering. The city herself becomes a person, weeping over her pain, screaming for aid, and protesting the deplorable conditions within her walls.[10] F. W. Dobbs-Allsopp describes the effect of this personification of Jerusalem. "By imbuing the city with personality and individuality, the poet gives his portrait of suffering the humanity and concreteness required to ring true to and to grip his audience. That is, it is one thing to look at a city in ruins, even if it is your own city, and quite another to imagine that city as a person who has suffered enormously."[11]

In the first two chapters of Lamentations, the city of Jerusalem is personified as a woman—a daughter and a mother. This female personification of the city evokes connotations of the pain and suffering of "a defiled woman" who, despite her grief and shame, survives against all odds.[12]

Even though Lamentations contains a clear sense of the reality of sin, the book also emphasizes the absolute pointlessness of suffering. This is particularly seen in the number of occasions where innocent children are depicted as starving and dying. Like no other, the image of children suffering and dying evokes strong emotions of the utter futility of war and destruction. The fact that Jerusalem is personified as a grieving mother transforms the images of the suffering children into "summary figures for the totality of the city's losses."[13] Particularly the dying children become a symbol of a future of the nation that is disintegrating as the people are watching.

In Lam 2 and 4, one finds an ironic reversal in reference to nursing language. The use of nursing language in these chapters stands in stark contrast to chapter 1 of this book, where God's provision of food was imaged in terms of nursing imagery, where the image of a mother nursing her child became the ultimate symbol of God's provision that is always there and always enough.

For instance, in Lam 2:11, the poet is terribly distressed about the destruction of Daughter Zion, which is ultimately connected to the plight of the babies and infants who are fainting in the streets of the city. It is ironic that the space where the children were supposed to be running around and playing as their parents conducted everyday business became a site of destruction. In verse 12 we read how the babies are dying from hunger at their mother's breast. Where the babies were supposed to find safety and life in their mother's bosoms, their life is now being poured out.

One cringes when one hears how innocent children cry in vain to their mothers for food to eat. The mothers, whose natural instinct is to provide for their children, are helpless and unable to feed their babies.

One finds here an indirect charge against God. The babies are not crying out for milk. In Lam 2:12, they call out for grain and wine because God is not providing food to the people. With no bread and no wine, the mothers' bodies cannot generate the necessary milk to nurse their children. Thus, God fails to feed the babies by withholding food from their mothers.

In Lam 4, nursing imagery is overturned to function as the ultimate symbol of when God does not feed. In Lam 4:3-4 this notion is graphically illustrated when Daughter Zion (in the Hebrew, lit. "the daughter of my people" [בת־עמי]) refuses to nurse her children. The babies are dying of thirst (literally, their tongues stick to the roofs of their mouths), and the children beg for food, but no one gives them anything to eat. Verse 3 states that Daughter Zion's actions are even worse than the animals considered to be cruelest of all, that is, the jackal (Isa 13:22; Mic 1:8) and the ostrich (Job 39:13-18).[14] There is no doubt that suffering can bring out the worst in people.

The most horrendous of all the images of God's failure to feed God's people is the image of mothers resorting to cannibalism (see also the tragic story told in 2 Kgs 6:26-30). In Lam 2:20, the shocking and outrageous question is asked whether women should have to eat their children (offspring) in order to survive. A play on words communicates the atrociousness of this image. The term for "their offspring" (פרים) literally means "fruit." The text wants to say that no mother should be in a situation where she has to eat her own children in order to survive, as casually as one would slice a pear. Thus, food imagery, which is supposed to symbolize enjoyment and nutrition, is used in a dreadful fashion to depict the ugly face of war and famine.

The image of cannibalism continues in Lam 4. Verse 10 narrates how compassionate mothers have boiled their children with their own hands to become food during the destruction of Daughter Zion. These women are not monsters. They are compassionate women, ordinary women who once rejoiced in the act of birth. But the unthinkable has happened. Mothers, who ordinarily would fight tooth and nail for the survival of their children and provide them with food—first from their own bodies and then by cooking nutritious meals—now use *their children* as ingredients for the same meals. This cannibalism may be more symbolic than actual, trying to capture some of the most desperate acts of desperate times in a few brush strokes. However, once more Lamentations points to the fact no woman, no one, should be forced to cannibalism in order to survive.[15]

In these images, there is the implicit, though frank, accusation against God for failing to feed God's children. Lamentations 2:20 bluntly asks how can God stand by and look while mothers are killing their children. But God is not just a passive onlooker. This is made clear from the accusation in verse 20, "to whom have you done this" harsh deed. Moreover, God's responsibility is suggested by a wordplay between the word for "children" (עֹלֲלֵי) and the word for God's act of abuse (עֹלַל) in this verse. God's complicity is further illustrated by the accusation in Lam 2:5 that God has become like an enemy. Prior to the images of babies dying of hunger and thirst, a violent picture is painted of God's destruction of the city. God is the overt subject of a series of verbs indicating destruction: God destroys, breaks down, brings down, and burns Daughter Judah. As a direct consequence of all of these acts, the city suffers from a severe famine so that babies die. One could say that God is directly responsible for the lack of food or, in other words, that God fails to feed God's people.

In light of this tragic state of affairs, what are we to do? In the presence of senseless suffering, it seems once more that sometimes there is nothing to do but lament. Accordingly, in Lam 2:18-20, Daughter Zion is urged to pour out her heart before God, to cry until she has no more tears left. Like Rachel in Jer 31:15, who weeps for her children and refuses to be comforted, she should do anything to get God's attention for the sake of her children who are dying of hunger. She begs God to acknowledge her situation, to notice the suffering of her children. Daughter Zion asks for nothing more than that God recognize her suffering, because "seeing and acknowledging pain can validate it." As Kathleen O'Connor so poignantly formulates it, "acknowledging pain is a form of embrace."[16]

We see some strong words of resistance contained in Lam 2:20-22. Daughter Zion poses a picture of a mother who draws the line and says, "Enough is enough." This mother sees a discrepancy between God's present role in the suffering of her children and her experience of God's care and nurture in the past. Therefore, she honestly confronts God with the hurt and pain experienced by her children. Frankly expressing her grief and anger, she questions the fairness of God's actions. In the process, she becomes a prime example of lamenting in the face of famine as radical suffering.

FAMINE AND HUMAN RESPONSIBILITY: WHEN PEOPLE ARE TO BLAME

Although singing laments and protesting before God concerning God's failure to feed is exceedingly important, it is not the whole story. We have to take seriously the role of human responsibility and sin in famine. The prophets typically made a connection between famine and human disobedience. In this regard, Birch argues that Joel understands the crisis of the locust plague as coming from God. In the face of this threat, the only hope for redemption is situated in the call for repentance.[17]

Accordingly, Joel sees the calamity of the famine caused by invading locusts as a sign of the imminent day of the Lord, when God will intervene in history. Whereas Israel normally saw the day of the Lord as a hopeful occasion when God would decisively defeat their enemies, Joel sees the day of the Lord as a day of judgment.[18] So terrifying is the prospect of having no food that Joel talks in cosmic proportions of the sun and moon darkening and darkness and gloom sweeping the land (Joel 2:10-11). This cosmic upheaval is described as the Garden of Eden becoming a wasting wilderness (v. 3).

In Joel 2:12-13, the prophet calls on the people to repent, to turn once more to God. They should turn from the path that leads to destruction and follow a path that will direct their steps on a road conducive to life. Joel calls people to hold a solemn gathering, where the whole community, young and old, and even the newlyweds are called to pray to God for mercy. However, Joel urges the people to engage not only in external acts of repentance, such as rending their clothing, but also internal acts, such as rending their hearts, thereby showing a deep inner response. Their only hope for salvation lies in God's character as gracious, merciful, patient, and loving (v. 13).

Amos 8 makes an even stronger connection between the role of human sin and the metaphor of God withholding food. The account of economic and social injustices in this chapter is shocking to say the least. In verse 6 we find that a human life is worth no more than a pair of sandals. Moreover, the people sell wheat that has fallen on the ground and has been soiled and trampled for a profit (v. 6). And verse 5 observes how the people have two sets of weights, one for buying and one for selling. All this is done out of greed, robbing the poor of income, dignity, and the right to make a living.[19]

The irony of the matter is that the people committing these offences are good religious people who kept the Sabbath and other religious festivals. But, while going about their religious activities, there is a restlessness among them to resume their illicit behavior. One could indeed call this greed disguised by religious pretense.

Amos warns his audience that this behavior will not go unpunished. In verse 8, God swears that the effects of their deeds will impact the earth like an earthquake hurling everything into turmoil. Thus, to distort justice has a certain and adverse effect on the earth and all of its inhabitants. God will further turn their festivals into ceremonies of mourning, with all the accompanying rituals. It will be as if the sun goes down in the middle of the day. And their crying will be as bitter as that of a family who has lost their only child. But the worst thing about this punishment is that God will be sending a famine of hearing the word of God. Amos's audience all knew the threat of famine, of having no food and water. But this famine of the word will be much worse than the devastation caused by lack of food and water. As a famine of food cuts off sustenance to the body, which eventually will cause the body to wither away, so the famine of the word causes the soul to suffer from malnutrition, which results in spiritual death. Nothing can be worse than being separated from God's word as the ultimate source of life (cf. Deut 8:3).

What makes this famine so severe is that people will desperately look everywhere, from sanctuary to sanctuary, from Dan to Beersheba (thus encompassing the whole of the country), but they will find no word from God, no guidance, no words of comfort. This will continue until even the most vigorous young men and women fall victim to this drought, employing the associations of a real drought to describe this spiritual famine. It is ironic that those who have refused to listen to God's word in the past are now punished by that same word being withheld from them.

Amos 8 does not have a happy ending. In verse 14 this sad fact is proclaimed: the people of Israel will fall never to rise again. History also tells us that the northern kingdom of Israel indeed ceased to exist. But the words were also addressed to a new generation in the southern kingdom, urging them not to make the same mistakes, to seriously contemplate their lives. And thousands of years later, new audiences are hearing the same words, urging them to reflect on their lives and to right the wrongs that are responsible for the suffering and pain in this world.

RESISTING FAMINE

In the previous sections, we have seen some disturbing images of the metaphor of God withholding food. Together they form an important countervoice that needs to be kept in balance within a biblical theological treatment of the metaphor of the God who feeds. Moreover, it is important to reflect on this dimension of God's failure to feed within a context of world famine today. For us Westernized, well-fed people, famine is something that may be completely foreign to us. Few of us have experienced as much as a day of going without food, not knowing where the next meal will come from. We are guarded by our wealth and, even in the worst-case scenario, government welfare. However, for a large percentage of the world population, hunger is all too real.

The two dimensions of the metaphor of God withholding food that have been introduced in this chapter, that is, famine as radical suffering and famine as human responsibility, each contribute a significant perspective concerning issues of theological reflection and human responsibility in the context of world famine. Actually, these two dimensions resemble what is happening in the world today concerning famine and starvation. First, world famine is simply a product of the development of life and civilization on our planet, a grievous problem for which some solution must be found, if at all possible. Famine and food scarcity is often caused by natural disasters, drought, crop failures, changing weather conditions, increased life span, and a rapid population growth.[20]

Second, one conceivably could think of famine on a different level, maybe helping us understand something of the suffering "lack" brings into our lives.[21] In this sense, famine would be those times when we feel as if everything that gives us life is destroyed or when we suffer from a lack of love, a lack of friendship, a lack of purpose, a lack of health, a lack of safety. Often we have as little control over these times of famine in our lives as Joel's audience had over the locusts that just kept on coming. We may lose a loved one due to death, or divorce, or illness; or a tragedy like September 11 may disrupt our lives. In situations such as these—when people find themselves in the midst of a terrible famine, in times where there is no food, no love, nothing—people sometimes have to accept that there is nothing any human can do to make things right. These are times when the only thing people can do is to turn to God and honestly express their hurt. Turning to God and expressing hurt are not passive acts. Rather, lament is a form of active resistance. As Samuel Balentine notes, "It is the very nature of lamentation to resist resignation and to press for change. Where there is lament, there is life, and even in the midst of suffering, this life will be vital and expectant."[22]

Something of this is clearly seen in the book of Lamentations. Despite the horrors the speakers are voicing, the mere fact that they are still able to sing laments signifies that they are still alive. Accordingly, Lamentations becomes a *testimony of survival*. In his book with the fitting title, *Surviving Lamentations*, Tod Linafelt argues that even though the inhabitants of Jerusalem are living the nightmare, they have survived the calamity. In the midst of the description of famine and death, one finds some rays of hope, some specks of life, something that indeed could be called "Surviving Lamentations."[23] The implicit message is that grief, no matter how devastating, is ultimately survivable.

In the process, something happens to the speakers. It is true that their suffering will not necessarily be changed by their cries, but in lamenting, they resist suffering by refusing to succumb to what life throws at them. Dobbs-Allsopp describes this resistance in terms of the book of Lamentations. "Lamentations stubbornly holds onto life and manifests a will to live that comes from knowledge of (or the belief in) tomorrow. Death and suffering are found throughout these remarkable poems, but they stand, for the most part, as 'memory's beginning,' not life's end."[24]

Zion fully embodies this notion. She is a woman hurt and hurting, but in her confrontation with God about the wrongness of that suffering, she comes across as a woman who is "defiantly alive" and will not be beaten down.[25]

The resistance exhibited by Daughter Zion in Lamentations strongly resembles protest theology, what is called antitheodicy in postholocaust circles. Antitheodicy can be described as "any religious response to the problem of evil whose proponents refuse to justify, explain, or accept as somehow meaningful the relationship between God and suffering."[26] Although antitheodicy can potentially be considered as being blasphemous, "the bite of antitheodicy's sting depends fundamentally on a persistent and stubborn love for God."[27]

A good example of this tendency is found in the short story, *Yosl Rakover Talks to God*.[28] The story is told of how Yosl Rakover finds himself in the dying moments of the Warsaw uprising in the Second World War. He has seen his wife and children die, together with thousands of his fellow Jewish people. He knows that he will not see another sunrise and, in the last few hours of his life, he writes a letter to God. In this letter, Yosl Rakover minces no words when he talks to God. He voices his anger and frustration, saying things like "[God] made me lower than the dust, tormented me to death, abandoned me to shame and mockery." He admonishes God for hiding his face, for allowing this terrible suffering to happen, saying, "And so my God, before I die, freed from all fear, beyond terror, in a state of absolute inner peace and trust, I will allow myself to call You to account one last time in my life.... God, I wish to ask You.... What more, O tell us, what more must happen before You reveal Your face to the world again?"[29]

Similarly, Lamentations functions as a protest against God for failing to feed God's people. Believers boldly ask about God's role in times of famine. Truth be told, one cannot help feeling a sense of disquiet about the understanding of God that is displayed in the metaphor of God withholding food or destroying the very creation God brought into being. One is left with the question whether one can worship an abusing God?[30]

The notion of an abusing God is worked out with particular clarity by David Blumenthal in *Facing the Abusing God*. Blumenthal argues that the Bible does indeed portray God as abusive. Nowhere is this more evident than in texts where God is portrayed as an abusive husband who sexually abuses Israel and then takes her back in love (Ezek 16:6-8; Hos 2:12, 21-22). Blumenthal's work seriously considers the question of God's responsibility in the Holocaust, or one could also say God's responsibility in times of famine. The question is asked whether God was "active, inactive, indirectly active, present, absent, silent, angry, powerless, punitive."[31]

To protest openly God's part in the times of famine is important for a number of reasons. First, one has to agree with Blumenthal that abusive behavior is inexcusable, in all circumstances. This relates to the antitheodic tendency to refuse to find reasons for God's actions. Under no circumstances can one justify abusive behavior—not in humans and definitely not in God. On the other hand, it is true that God is depicted in the biblical traditions as abusive, but not always. Although this violent imagery for God is an undeniable part of the scriptural witness of God and therefore cannot be ignored, these images cannot be treated in isolation from other language about God. God is also loving and kind.[32] Although God is indeed portrayed as withholding food in times of famine, which may indeed be construed as abusive, there is more than enough evidence that God is also the God who graciously feeds all of creation.

Second, to protest God's role in withholding food honestly, and thereby voicing one's anger and pain, is *psychologically* exceedingly important. As Walter Brueggemann states: "Only grief permits newness. Without lament, hope is stillborn."[33] For the healing process to work, it is crucial to admit, understand, and cope with our feelings of anguish, remorse, fury, protest, and hatred—even against God. The importance of a book like Lamentations is that it provides a healthy model for dealing with suffering "by creating space for grief and teaching how to grieve"— a model of living that is vitally important for contemporary communities of faith.[34]

Finally, *theologically* Daughter Zion's example of voicing anger and pain in times of famine is also significant. The example of believers who have honestly expressed their anger to God says something important about their relationship with God. Antitheodicy fundamentally means that people still address God. Even though they accuse God of being absent and even of afflicting them, they are still speaking to God. Thus, they are very different from the atheist who ignores God. They are honest in their relationship with God and feel free to voice their anger. And their anger shows that they have not let go of God. They still fervently believe in God. As Yosl Rakover says: "I am saying all this to You in plain words because I believe in You, because I believe in You more than ever before, because I know now that You are my God."[35] They hold fast to the faith that, despite the hopelessness of the situation, God is still a God of goodness and justice who wills life rather than death for creation. And therefore, they continue to cry out to God because of God's apparent absence and silence, hoping that God will once more look favorably on them.

ACCEPTING RESPONSIBILITY

On the other hand, Sallie McFague's claim is very true. She says, "If God is absent from this world, it is because we are."[36] Made in God's image, we are supposed to serve as God's hands and feet in the world. Once more focusing on the role of human responsibility in world famine, one is urged by the millions of human beings dying of starvation to ask questions such as, Who is dying at whose cost?

Although it would be dangerous to ascribe all misfortune to human sin (the example of Job is a good reminder), there is an important element of truth in the prophetic perspective that made a connection between famine and human responsibility. It is true that there is a link between today's world hunger and people's disobedience.[37] Famine happens where people fail. Overeating and overconsumption, gross inequality in the control of wealth, the exploitation of the natural resources of the earth, and a desire to maintain one's own lifestyle at the expense of the poor clearly constitute sin in the biblical perspective. The irony of the matter is that those who are most responsible for world hunger are the ones who escape its ravages. It is the innocent and the helpless who suffer, who most often feel that God does not feed.

In our own lives, we have to be candid and admit that sometimes when we experience times of famine in our personal lives, we are also responsible in some fashion or another. When relationships go wrong, when our health fails, when we experience failure at work, sometimes we have only ourselves to blame. We are humans who make mistakes. To realize our contribution to the misery of others is a crucial first step. For instance, in terms of world famine, we are all guilty, participating in consumerism, buying clothes made by laborers of the Third World who are paid less than a dollar an hour. Alan B. Durning gives the following examples of people's liability in his report on poverty for the Worldwatch Institute:

> Americans spend five billion dollars each year on special diets to lower their calorie consumption, while 400 million people around the world are so undernourished, their bodies and minds are deteriorating. As water from a single spring in France is bottled and shipped to the prosperous around the globe, nearly two billion people drink and bathe in water contaminated with deadly parasites and pathogens.[38]

Oftentimes in response to this reality, people end up doing nothing. This apathy may be due to some people being blind to the plight of those people near and far who suffer need in various aspects of their lives. Alternatively, others who are aware of these social concerns may be so paralyzed by the magnitude of the problem that they also fail to act.

Yet, we are called to repent, to admit the part we play in creating famine in the world. We are called to resist suffering. There are things to be done to ensure that God will feed again. To name two things: First, focusing on the role humans play in resisting famine, there is much people can do to diminish evil in the world, to lessen the gap between the haves and the have-nots. Farley argues that compassion plays a crucial role in resisting suffering by providing help to the helpless, "food for the hungry, jobs for the homeless, medicine for the sick," which she calls, "sacraments of compassion's care."[39] But it is not enough just to nurse the wounds. True compassion seeks to go to the heart of the matter, empowering people to resist injustice and fight for liberation from everything that limits quality of life.

Something of this compassion is evident in Lamentations where it initially looks as if there is no one to be found to comfort Daughter Zion in her misery. Even God, whom one would expect would provide comfort, is actually responsible for the situation in which Zion finds herself. Even though Zion calls out to God, asking God to see her plight, God never answers. In the book of Lamentations, God never comforts Daughter Zion, never sees her suffering. But Daughter Zion has a comforter after all. In Lam 2, the narrator sees her pain, hears her laments, cries with her, and calls on her to express her innermost hurt and anger. The narrator shares her pain and, in the process, offers her back some sense of her dignity.[40] What's more, the narrator's act of compassion encourages the reader to also feel Daughter Zion's pain.

It is true that already through technology, foreign aid, and charity, many people have received basic medical care, education, and a better standard of living. For instance, private organizations like Food for the Hungry and Bread for the World have achieved some success in reducing world hunger. A survey conducted by the Food and Agriculture Organization from 1969 and 1971 estimated that 918 million people had inadequate access to food. The 1990–1992 World Food survey estimated the number to be 841 million. The decline in the number of people who suffer from lack of food over the past twenty years is extraordinary when one considers that the world population has increased by 1.5 billion during the same period.[41] However, there are still too many people who shirk their responsibility and who suffer from complacency, feeling powerless in light of all that needs to be done. Nevertheless, as in the case of Daughter Zion, one person can make a whole lot of difference.

Second, to express one's pain honestly before God is based on the assumption that God is able to make a difference, that God *will* feed again. In a Jewish midrash, *Lamentations Rabbah*, one sees how the believers' laments are not in vain. The story is told of how the patriarchs call a heavenly trial where they put God on trial for the suffering of Israel. First, Abraham demands to know why God has singled Israel out in this terrible suffering. Then Moses reprimands God for God's silence when so many mothers and children died in the same day. But it is Rachel who finally gets through to God. Rachel is calling God to have compassion on her children out of her own example. She, who is Rachel, was not envious of her rival, Leah. Why then should God be jealous of idolatry and cause Rachel's children to go into exile and to be slain by the sword? It is finally Rachel's own advocacy for her children and her refusal to be comforted, as quoted in the prooftext of Jer 31:15, that finally causes God's mercy to well up. As the midrash says: "Then God was stirred, and said: 'For thy sake Rachel, I will restore Israel to their place'" (*Lam. Rab.* 24).[42] The midrash wants to say that like Rachel, Mother Zion pleads for her children. And Mother Zion's pleas will equally not be in vain. The destruction of the city of Jerusalem with its people and the radical suffering of famine do not yield the last word.

This leads us to the notion of *hope*. Tod Linafelt has done imaginative work on the afterlife of Lamentations. He says that in light of the fact that God never responds to Daughter Zion's suffering in the book of Lamentations and that Lam 2 ends with the image of all Zion's children who have been brought to an end it may seem in times of famine as if there is no hope at all. But as Linafelt's title suggests, something in this text kept on surviving, kept on living, so that other later texts, for example, *Lamentations Rabbah*, would feel the urge to provide God's missing response.[43] A few decades later, another prophet spoke some words of hope. Isaiah 48–54 keeps Zion alive and provides her with a beautiful future. Her family life is restored. For instance, in Isa 49:15, God assumes the persona of a mother. God speaks directly to her, comforts her, and promises to return her children to her.[44] This is something that will also be seen in the next chapter where God's provision of food is used as a symbol of restoration.

WHEN A MOTHER FAILS TO FEED

In imagining the metaphor of God withholding food in female terms, one has some options to be creative. Particularly in Lamentations, there is a striking female presence. These images could be used as a point of departure in imagining the other gender-neutral texts dealing with God's failure to feed her children in female terms.

In Lam 2 and 4, one saw tragic pictures of the suffering of mothers not being able to provide food to their children, neither from their own bodies, nor from the resources to cook nutritious meals. Whereas an image of nursing was in some texts considered to be one of the best examples to describe God's nurture and care in reference to the provision of food, the image of mothers not being able to nurse is heartbreaking. Not to be able to provide food to your children goes against the most basic instinct of mothers. Moreover, one also sees how Daughter Zion, who is personified as a mother, becomes the ultimate symbol of a mother's suffering. It seems as if the mothers' failure to provide food to their children in Lam 2 and 4 is paralleled by Mother Zion who in a way also fails to feed the children of Jerusalem when the raging famine depletes the city's food resources. If one extends this analogy, one conceivably could say that, within the metaphor of God failing to feed God's people, God is also portrayed as a mother unable to provide food.

But even worse than mothers unable to feed their children is where these same compassionate mothers resort to cannibalism in order to survive. This shocking imagery parallels the abusive imagery that is used to describe God's actions against the city. As the mothers fail to feed their children and engage in violent acts too disturbing to imagine, so God destroys her own. One could venture to say that God is portrayed as a "compassionate mother" who has resorted to the worst possible abuse.

In Lam 2, we have seen how God is held responsible and openly accused for God's failure to feed. Daughter Zion is urged to express her anger and grief honestly. She begs God to see her misery. And in *Lam. Rab.* 24, another mother, Rachel, pleads with God to have compassion. One could say in these instances that one mother is begging another to understand and help. This beautiful contemporary prayer expresses this idea.

> Ruler of the Universe
> I Sarah, daughter of Ruth, come before You as a mother.
> When my child is sick,
>   I care for her with all my soul and with all my body.
> I use my lips to recite prayer for her.
> I use my legs to fetch good foods to sustain her.
> I use my voice to sing her soothing songs.
> I use my hands to hold her close.
> And You, Who are the Creator of all flesh
>   and the Mother of Your people Israel,

> What have You done to soothe Your children
>   who are sick with longing for Jerusalem?
> You have given us life and Your slightest movement
>   would be enough to sustain and nourish that life.
> How can You withhold that help
>   and not be shamed before Your children?[45]

This protest is based on the basic belief that God in God's very nature is still gracious, merciful, patient, compassionate, and able to deliver and bring life out of death. When singing their laments, people believed that God, the ultimate source of deliverance, was able to change their circumstances. Farley describes this notion:

> God is infinitely compassionate and tender toward the world. Suffering comes because our bodies are frail and because human beings can be cruel to one another—individually and through institutional structures. God labors night and day, like a mother comforting a delirious child, to soothe the fever, to penetrate the suffering and despair. Nothing separates God from the world, but suffering can be a veil that hides this loving presence. In the midst of suffering, compassion labors to tear the veil.[46]

Almost always there is a note of hope that God will hear, that God can break the famine, that God will give food again. God is like a mother who not only understands pain but also weeps because of it and toils nonstop to ease the suffering.

Within a feminist theological interpretation of God's failure to feed, one should be aware of a number of dangers. First, in Lamentations it is only the mothers who are resorting to cannibalism. To make only mothers responsible for withholding food may have the adverse consequence of scapegoating, that is, instilling the notion that women are evil.[47] However, the reason for using this image may be the same reason why the image of a mother nursing was thought to be such a good example to describe God's provision of food in chapter 1. The image of mothers unable to feed their children and, instead, resorting to eat these same children, illustrates the ultimate reversal of the image.

Second, parents and educators alike tell us about the danger of using food as punishment. To withhold food from children may generate negative connotations concerning food that actually may lead to eating disorders. Accordingly, Kim Chernin has described the identity struggle that results from food and the mother who provides it—a classic example being of the mother (and father) who tells their child, "You will sit here until you have finished your meal." Chernin notes that what really is occurring in this interaction is a heated debate about identity.[48]

To use food as punishment is particularly a problem in terms of maternal language for God. The reason for this is that psychologists like Melanie Klein have argued that there seems to be an integral connection between food, identity, and the mother. Already in the infant stage, the child is both symbiotically dependent on her mother through the act of nursing but, at the same time, tries to individuate herself from her mother. This relationship between food, identity, and the mother continues as the child grows, which could create all kinds of psychological problems if the mother uses food as a means of punishment (or reward).[49] Thus, to portray God as a Mother who withholds food as punishment raises a unique set of problems, which manifests itself in the complex relationship of children being dependent on their Mother but, at the same time, trying to find their own identity.

Third, the image of God as a Mother using food as punishment raises questions as to how to deal with the image of God as abusive Mother. One has to realize that an abusive God, whether male or female, is problematic. In Lam 2, it is ironic that Daughter Zion is urged to turn for help and healing to God, who was responsible for her abuse (Lam 2:18-20). If one continues to imagine God as a Mother who withholds food, one could envisage Zion as an abused daughter in a codependent relationship with her abusive Mother. The notion of an abused and violated woman turning for help to her abuser is troubling indeed. Even though she does this for the lives of her children who faint of hunger—and one thus sees something of a mother who will do *anything* to save her children—this portrayal remains disturbing. An abusive, dominating, and manipulating mother could do as much harm as an abusive spouse.[50]

Probably, one needs to accept on some level that one cannot "save" these troubling images. But on the other hand, the notion that God is abusive, but not always, rings true. There is enough biblical evidence that God is still the same loving Mother as before, leading believers to challenge God to be true to her own nature. A first step would be to be honest about the problems associated with this aspect of the metaphor of God's provision of food and to highlight the many instances where the opposite is true about God. Ultimately, the only thing one can do is live with this tension.

In the next chapter, we will see how even in the midst of their suffering, Israel kept the hope alive that God will feed again. We will see how the metaphor of the God who feeds starts to move into the realm of the eschatology, in which visions of restoration are used to imagine what God's provision of food is supposed to be.

CHAPTER 4

THE MOUNTAINS SHALL DRIP SWEET WINE .

Visions of Restoration

In our exploration of the metaphor of the God who feeds, one dimension that is striking to say the least is Israel's unwavering hope that God will feed again. Even in the darkest of times, Israel still believed that famine was not the last word. Accordingly, in a number of prophetic texts, visions of restoration follow visions of famine and judgment.

Israel's belief in the new life that lies ahead is expressed in many diverse voices. For instance, Jeremiah's Little Book of Comfort (Jer 30–31), Ezekiel's rather surreal visions (e.g., the vision of dry bones in Ezek 37 and the newly restored Jerusalem in Ezek 40–48), and the vibrant poetry of Isa 40–55 all provide different visions of a future in which God will restore Israel's fortunes. The poets of these texts indeed used multiple images and metaphors to describe God's restoration of Israel, expressing the idea that no one image is able to capture the "lyrical, imaginative, and exuberant" nature of the imagined future.[1] Often these images applied older traditions in a new way to underscore the fact that their hope for the future was solely situated in God's past providence and faithfulness. For instance, in Isa 43:16-17, the restoration is imaged in terms of a new exodus, where God will make a way through the sea and lead God's people back home. Additionally, the idea of a new creation is a recurring theme in these restoration texts. Central to the notion of the redemption of the people lies the restoration and renewal of all of creation. In Isa 41:18-20, God transforms the natural world by bringing rivers and pools of water in the wilderness and by planting an array of trees in the desert (see also Isa 43:19-20). In the same way, Israel's memory of the God who fed God's children in the wilderness is also picked up again and employed in different ways to describe their hope for the future. Accordingly, we will see in this chapter how restoration is expressed with the metaphor of God who will once more provide food in abundance.

In the first section, God's provision of food relates to the hope that God will change Israel's immediate future. In the following two sections, the metaphor of God who will feed again is described in hyperbolic terms, surpassing what would have been considered normal food production. Donald Gowan notes that most scholars distinguish these extraordinary visions of the future from the "ordinary hopes for a better future by calling them 'eschatology.'" Gowan points out that although the term *eschatology* could be understood in terms of the doctrine about the "end," or the "last things," the Old Testament does not formally deal with the end of the world, or time, or history. Rather the Old Testament expresses the hope for a better future in terms of God's transformation of the terrible wrongs of this world to constitute a new age characterized by order and peace.[2] In the following sections, we will see how the eschatological understanding of God's provision of food is rooted squarely in the belief that God will change the situation of famine in the here and now.

When God Feeds Again

For Israel to say that God will feed again meant that they believed a time would come when they could rebuild their lives. They imagined such a time to be something like the following: After an excruciating period of having no food to eat, the Israelites once again will have enough food to satisfy all of their needs. There is peace in the land so that the people are in a situation of being able to plant their fields and enjoy the fruits of their harvest. This hope is expressed in theological terms when they regard God as the primary actor of their restored fortunes. They believed in a God who, as we have seen in some of the earlier chapters, fed them in the wilderness like a mother feeding her child and who graciously provides to all of creation. Even when these people experienced terrible times of famine, they still held fast to their belief in the Gracious Provider and called upon God to change their situation.

Similarly, in the following three visions of restoration, we will see how God continues to be the One who will restore the people's fortunes by yet again providing food.

In Jer 31:11-14, God's deliverance of Judah is expressed in terms of a God who will once more provide the grain, wine, oil, and newborn flock, which is described in verse 12 as "the goodness of God." This gift of food has the effect of transforming their lives to be like "a watered garden," which will never again whither because of drought. Jeremiah 31:13 clearly states that it is God who is responsible for this new situation when God turns their mourning into joy, comforts them, and brings them happiness.

In Amos 9:13-15, God's activity is described in typical restoration language, "I will restore the fortunes of my people" (v. 14; see also Jer 29:14; Jer 30:3; Ezek 16:53). In this text, God is the explicit subject of the restoration, whose activity of restoring the people to their land allows them to engage in their ordinary activities of building houses, planting vineyards and gardens, and consequently eating and drinking from the harvests. Verse 15 uses an agricultural metaphor to describe God's action. Here God will "plant" the people in the land that is a gift from God, ensuring that they will never be plucked up again. The people will not only share in the abundance of the land but also be an intricate part of it, becoming one of the bountiful crops that is planted in the land.

Finally, Joel 2:18-19 describes God as having pity on God's people. In response to Israel's laments, God is sending them grain, wine, and oil. This act of God is a direct reversal of the anguish described in Joel 1:10. Further, Joel 2 notes how God's activity of restoration enables the people to engage in agricultural activities, or one could say *how* God feeds again. For instance, in verse 20, God does great things by removing the threat of the enemy invasion, thereby creating a safe environment for the people to sow again and to replant their vineyards and gardens. Moreover, in verse 23, we see how God is jubilantly praised for giving more than enough rain—the early and later rain that creates the perfect environment for a good harvest.

In each of these three texts, the appalling famine imagery of chapter 3 is overturned. We will see from the following description how God's renewed provision of food picks up some of the same themes that featured earlier in this book in order to portray the new era in the life of Israel. In addition to continuing the original metaphor, we also see how these restoration texts confer a unique flavor to the way in which God's provision of food serves as a symbol of restoration.

First, the hope that God will feed again is painted in *magnificent terms*. Joel 2:24-26 depicts God's provision of food as greatly satisfying and abundant. The grain bins and the storing vats for the newly pressed wine will not be large enough to hold all the food that God provides. There is an interesting wordplay in verses 25-26. Instead of the locusts "eating" (אכל Joel 1:4; 2:25) and the fire "eating" (אכלה Joel 1:19-20) their crops, Judah now will eat and be perfectly satisfied (cf. the series of infinitive absolutes ואכלתם אכול ושבוע in v. 26). In Amos 9, this superfluity is depicted in even stronger terms. Verse 13 describes God's provision of food in hyperbolic terms when the land will be so fertile that crops will be planted even before the harvest has been brought in. One thus sees that God, when God feeds again, does so in no small measure. Israel believed that, after all the years of scarcity, a time would come when they would have more than enough food to eat.

Second, the abundance of God's renewed provision of food is reason for celebration. Once more the theme of *joy* forms a central aspect of this envisioned restoration. In Joel 2:21-23, the earth and all of her inhabitants are called to be happy and rejoice because of the food that God once more has supplied. Whereas the children of Zion were urged to lament in Joel 1 (vv. 5, 8, 11, 13), they now are invited to praise God for their promising future.

This emphasis on joy is even more striking in the restoration text of Jer 31:12-13, where people shall come and exuberantly sing aloud over God's goodness, which is manifested in God's renewed provision of food. As verse 13 states, young women shall be joyous and dance, together with the young and the old, for God will turn their mourning into joy. God will comfort them and give them gladness instead of sorrow.

Third, a central aspect of God's renewed provision of food is that *all* of creation shares in the joy. We saw in chapter 2 how God provides food to all of creation. And in chapter 3, Joel 1 dramatically illustrates how the whole earth (v. 10) and all the animals (v. 18) lament over the terrible famine. It is thus quite appropriate that God's restoration also extends to all of God's creation. As a result, Joel 2:21 addresses the earth, speaking words of comfort to her and encouraging her to be joyful and rejoice about the great deeds that God has done. Also the animals that once groaned are now called to rejoice in verse 22, for they too have received gifts of food when the dry land was transformed into green pastures and the fruit trees became full with fruit.

Fourth, God's provision of food serves as an illustration of *God's presence*. This is most evident in Joel 2:22-27, where the effect of the detailed description of God's renewed provision of sufficient and satisfying food is to let people know that God is in the midst of Israel. The food that now graces their tables again will cause the people to recognize the Giver as their God, that there is no other (v. 27).

The notion of God's presence is developed further in verses 28-29 where God's spirit is poured out upon all flesh. These verses are linked to the previous section in order to provide tangible evidence of God's abiding presence. As in Ezek 37, where the Spirit formed a crucial element in restoring the people's lives (seen very literally when the Spirit gives life to skeletons), the Spirit becomes in Joel 2 a sign of the new life that God will give to all flesh. God's presence will manifest itself in visible signs of dreams, prophecies, and visions—ways in which God communicates with God's people. Once more this restoration is all-inclusive, extending to every member of the restored community, young, old, male and female, even slaves. Thus, all distinctions of gender, age, and even social position are immaterial in the new community that will be characterized by God's presence.

This description of God's presence, which is dramatically expressed in Joel 2, is something that has been featured in some fashion throughout this book. Chapter 1 portrayed God's provision of food as a sign of God's presence or, one could say, as a sign of God's attentive nature. God's presence stands in stark contrast to the experience of God's absence or God's hostile presence that was typical of the famine imagery discussed in chapter 3. In light of famine resulting from drought or war, one could well imagine that for those who experienced such food scarcity restored food resources were one of the surest signs of God's restored favor.

Finally, Israel regarded this future hope as such a sure thing because Joel speaks of it as if already accomplished by repeatedly using the perfect verbal form (an indication that the action is completed) to describe the ensuing restoration: God *has* given the rain (v. 23), the threshing floor *is* full of grain, and the vat *is* overflowing with wine (v. 24). The hope that God will feed again is so sure that the poet describes it as something that has already taken place (see also the infinitive absolutes used in v. 26 "you shall eat abundantly and be satisfied"). Even whereas people may still have experienced pangs of hunger, and their future looked bleak, the people firmly believed in a God who will feed again.

The portrayal of God who will feed again as means of expressing the belief that God will restore Israel's fortunes becomes even more colorful and elaborate in the texts that describe God's provision of food in mythopoetic categories. For instance, the normalization of the food supply after a time of famine as seen in Joel 2:19-26 is enlarged in Joel 3:18 (4:18 MT) to reach miraculous proportions. We will see in the next section how a number of texts raise God's provision of food as a sign of restoration to a hyperbolic level, communicating something of a return to an almost paradisical state.

RETURN TO PARADISE

In Amos 9:13, the superabundance of God's provision of food naturally leads into a euphoric statement of there being so many grapes that the mountains shall drip with the newly pressed grape juice, and the hills shall flow with it. A very similar text is seen in Joel 3:18 (4:18 MT) when the earlier crisis that Joel 1 described is now reversed. The freshly pressed, not-yet fermented grape juice that was once cut off during the famine (1:5) now drips from the mountains. The cattle who earlier wandered about with no pasture to graze upon (1:18) now give milk in such large quantities that it flows from the hills.

These texts imagine a world where no hard labor is necessary to produce the necessary food: no ploughing, no planting, and no reaping. It is a world where one can just stand at the foot of the mountain with a little container, gathering as much milk and newly pressed wine as one's heart desires.

In this regard, Izak Cornelius argues that, although the notion of a garden that can be understood in paradisical terms does not occur in the prophetic books, one could talk of typical paradisical motifs that capture "the future idealistic situation of abundant fertility, cosmic harmony, life, bliss and peaceful tranquility," which stand in contrast with "chaos, infertility and death."[3] Cornelius notes that the eschatological hope that is at the heart of some of these restoration texts does not necessarily mean a return to the paradise that was lost ("Urzeit") but envisions a totally new situation that surpasses the initial paradise by far ("Endzeit").[4]

The hyperbolic depiction of God's provision of food elevates the metaphor to express something of this paradisical state. It may be that the current situation has incited the poet to look toward a future restoration, perhaps because their present circumstances were not relieved. It may be that people after the exile experienced natural disasters and economic depression, which only continued their former experience of food scarcity. Their hope of a new creation was thus transposed to a future where there will be most certainly enough to eat. Or maybe the poets so appreciated food after experiencing hunger for so long that they used God's provision of food to imagine God's final restoration. Either way, we see in these texts some of the same elements that were present in the first part of this chapter; however, the mythopoetic elements that are interweaved in this depiction bestow an ethereal quality to the metaphor of God who will feed again.

In this portrayal of God's renewed provision of food, the miraculous state of affairs is once more made possible by God alone who will do the impossible to restore Judah's fortunes. Joel 3 (4 MT) vividly depicts how God's abundant restoration of the food supplies is directly related to God removing the threat of enemies in order to create a safe environment. Accordingly, verses 11-14 describe how God will judge the neighboring nations, using a harvest metaphor where the abundance of wine becomes an ironic means of describing how the other nations will be crushed. God's judgment is directly responsible for the idyllic scene of the mountains dripping with wine.

Two themes underlie this metaphor of judgment. Verse 14 describes this judgment of the nations in terms of the "Day of the Lord." This day of God's judgment, which acts simultaneously as a day of salvation for Judah, exhibits cosmic proportions, as noted in verse 15, where the sun, moon, and stars will be darkened (cf. a similar description in Joel 2:30-32). Moreover, God's judgment is depicted in terms of the metaphor of the Divine Warrior, who will meet the enemies in a battle of cosmic proportions. Verse 10 expresses this metaphor by applying an expression that denotes a time of peace (cf. Mic 4; Isa 2) in a directly opposite manner to describe this cosmic battle with the enemy, "Beat your plowshares into swords, / and your pruning hooks into spears." Even the weakest member of the nation is to think of himself as a warrior and take part in the battle led by God.[5]

In the midst of this turmoil, God promises to be a refuge and a fortress for the people of Israel (v. 16; cf. Ps 46:1-3). And after the enemy is defeated, we see in verse 17 how God dwells in Zion, echoing ancient Near Eastern traditions that the deity is enthroned victoriously in his mountain abode after the cosmic battle, which is then followed by a string of blessings that causes the nature to burst forth with fruitfulness and plentiful harvests.[6] God's miraculous provision of food is thus made possible by God the warrior who will forcefully remove the enemies to create a paradisical state of peace and well-being.

For a modern reader who is aghast at the atrocities of war and the senseless suffering of innocent victims of war, the Divine Warrior imagery that is used in this text is problematic to say the least. In this regard, one needs to realize that the prophet is speaking to his own people, who are seeing themselves as extremely vulnerable and overpowered by the super-powers around them. For people who have been ravaged by war, a text such as Joel 3 could provide some sense of a future hope when God will face the violent forces that threaten to engulf them. Although the Divine Warrior imagery is designed to portray a God who is capable of counter-ing the most tyrannical powers, such imagery should not be applied uncritically in a time where violence can have disastrous effects. However, one can look through the violence and see how this vision expresses something of the belief that God is present in the midst of our worst fears.

Finally, we see how God's provision of food affects all creation. The oracle in Joel 3:18 culminates with the vision of a river, gushing forth from the house of God, that will revive the thirsty land (see also Ps 46:4; 65:9). In one breath, the poet describes how wine and milk will run down the mountains, which are subsequently connected to a vitalizing river bringing water into a parched land. One sees in this depiction how God's presence will lead to all kinds of material benefits for people as well as for all creation. Thus, in the same way as the natural order is transformed, so God's miraculous provision of food becomes a striking symbol of God's restoration.

This idea of a life-giving stream that flows from Zion, and more specif-ically from the sanctuary to revive the rest of the land, is vividly portrayed in the restoration text of Ezek 47. In this text, a stream of water flows from the sanctuary. When it reaches the "sea of stagnant waters," or the Dead Sea, the waters miraculously lose their high saline content and become fresh. This river is truly life-giving as evidenced in verse 9, where it is emphasized that everything will live wherever the river goes.[7] Thus, the river will water the dry desert and bring life along its path. The

Judean desert and the Dead Sea, a pinnacle of barren environments, serve as a dramatic reminder of the restoration that will occur.

In addition, the river is full of all kinds of fish that are caught by people fishing next to the river. And on both sides of the river, there is a great variety of trees, which never lose their leaves and which bear fruit all through the year—a new fruit each month. In this image of restoration, one sees an extraordinary change from a desolate spot to a paradise.

Moreover, this river is not only giving life wherever it goes, it also provides food by means of fish and fruit trees, which further add to the river's life-giving quality. It is important to note that the water from the river originates in the temple, which is considered to be the home of God, as suggested by the city's name "God is there" (יהוה שמה Ezek 48:35).[8] In light of the fact that the river directly originates from God, one could say that God feeds all the inhabitants of the land by means of the fruit trees that grow next to the river and the fish that the river supplies. There are once more clear associations of life with God's provision of food. Since the river flows from God's sanctuary and provides life-giving food, one can make the connection between the water flowing from God's city and the food that God provides as showing how God's provision of food is an essential expression of God's presence.

Once more there is a sense of abundance related to God's provision of food, as illustrated by the emphasis on the great variety of fish, as well as the uninterrupted supply of fruit from the fruit trees next to the river. Not only is there a constant supply of food, but the leaves of the trees have an additional function as indicated by the remark in verse 13: they are good for healing. This medicinal quality of the trees adds to the notion that the river that flows from the sanctuary gives life. Or one could say that the God who feeds also heals what is broken—an apt metaphor for a people who have experienced the worst suffering possible.

An interesting side note is to be found in the reference in verse 11. The swamps and marshes associated with the Dead Sea will not become fresh but will be left for salt. This aside may suggest that even though God's life-giving source provides fresh water, which is essential for life, taste is not unimportant. Salt is an essential spice for creating tasty dishes, indicating that God's provision of food is pleasant and supposed to be enjoyed—something that is understood by the regular associations with joy with regard to God's provision of food. This is also something that we will see in the next section, when one of the ultimate expressions of God's provision of food is the feast or banquet.

LIFE AS A BANQUET

Israel's belief that God will feed again also became a way of speaking about God's final restoration. In what is often called the Isaianic Apocalypse (Isa 24–27), one sees the final redemption of God's people depicted in terms of God hosting a glorious banquet on Mount Zion, symbolizing a time of peace that follows upon God removing the threat of enemies forever. As in the texts that were presented in the previous section, mythopoetic terms image God's provision of food; however, in the case of Isa 24–27, the restoration seems to be even more lustrous, painted with bright colors.

As the title of Patrick Miller's article suggests, themes of judgment and joy are present throughout Isa 24–27.[9] As in the previous section, this new era of peace, introduced as a consequence of God's judging activity, describes a new creation. God's judgment and destruction of God's enemies are the means of "redoing things, by tearing down and starting over." After the cosmic conflict with the earthly and supernatural powers, Isa 25:6-8 states that the Lord of hosts now reigns on Mount Zion. On this mountain, God will thus reveal God's presence by hosting a festival to celebrate this victory over the forces of chaos. Dan Johnson expresses this view by saying, "Yahweh will reign on Mount Zion. Chaos will return to cosmos. And the golden age will have arrived."[10]

The text images this "golden age" as a banquet, an ongoing meal where God is the host who presents "a feast of rich food, a feast of well-aged wines" (v. 6b). The rich food literally means "fat foods," and although "fatty foods" do not have the same connotations for health-conscious Westerners, these foods, which are prepared with a lot of oil, were considered to be a delicacy. Moreover, the emphasis on the "well-aged" quality of the wines emphasizes that these wines had time to be preserved, in contrast to new wine that one would have expected to drink after everything was destroyed during the enemy invasion. The second part of verse 6 explains this festival further, where it says that the fat dishes are filled with marrow. The detailed description of the meal that God will provide indicates the five-star quality of the food.

This banquet with food aplenty, and not ordinary food but the most luxurious foods imaginable, is a fitting culmination of the metaphor of the God who feeds. It makes sense that if the poets had to imagine a time when God would conquer enemy forces that constantly threatened them and jeopardized their food supply, a good way to illustrate this gift of peace and life would be by imagining a rich, ongoing banquet where everybody has enough to eat.

This banquet and all it symbolizes is reason for celebration. Continuing the associations between joy and God's provision of food, joy plays a central role in the depiction of this eschatological banquet. By means of a radical restoration, the joy that was said in Isa 24:11 to have gone into exile, now has returned with, what Miller calls, an "interruptive joy that erupts and cannot be contained."[11] For example, in Isa 25:1-5, the community praises God spontaneously for God's victory over the chaos that had disrupted their lives for so long (also 26:1-6). The wine that dried up and the vine that languished in Isa 24:7 are now restored to bring forth an abundance of wine that miraculously had time to be preserved. Thus, after all the years in which there was no wine to drink and no songs to sing (Isa 24:9), people now will exuberantly sing songs of praises, be glad, and rejoice in God's salvation (Isa 25:9).

It is important to note that God is preparing this sumptuous banquet for *all* people (see the five-fold repetition of "all" in vv. 6-8). Israel imagined their restored life with God as a banquet where the whole community eats together. A central question that has occupied people throughout the centuries is who is invited to this table. As Johnson notes, questions of universalism versus particularism are dispersed throughout this text. He argues that universal references to "all peoples," "all nations," "all faces," and "all the earth" are alternated with the particular notions of "this mountain," "his people," and "our God."[12] It seems as if God's actions on behalf of God's people, Israel, will benefit not only the community of Israel but also all the peoples of the earth. We will later see how some postbiblical interpretations interpreted Isa 25 in reference to the question, who is included in this eschatological vision?

As in chapter 2, God's provision of food as a symbol of restoration contains a strong element of justice. Right before the banquet that God hosts for all people (Isa 25:4), God acts as a refuge to the poor and needy in their distress. Using images from weather conditions that would have been considered especially threatening to those who are in need, God provides shelter from a thunderstorm and shade from the scorching sun. God's final restoration is therefore genuinely inclusive, extending particularly to the poor and needy. We can confidently assume that the banquet that God hosts will also provide food to those who need it most. The words of Ps 22:26 (27 MT) echo something of this sentiment: "The poor shall eat and be satisfied; / those who seek him shall praise the LORD."

Although this vision of Isa 25 provides one of the most wonderfully inclusive visions in the Old Testament, one should be careful not to overly romanticize this universal perspective. Right after "all the people" are invited to the banquet hosted by God, it seems that "all" people are not really "all." This becomes clear in verses 10-12 where Moab is wholeheartedly excluded and wished a gruesome end.[13] Nevertheless, one does see how the book of Ruth makes an important corrective on this prohibition where a Moabite, Ruth, is included in what Katharine Doob Sakenfeld calls the "peaceable community."[14]

Adding a whole new dimension to God's provision of food is that this newly restored age cannot be fully established until every threatening force is removed. Isaiah 25:7 states that on God's mountain, God will swallow the covering that envelops all peoples. By taking away the shrouds or masks from the faces of the people, God is not only removing but also destroying all evidence of mourning. This notion continues in verse 8, which tells us that God will wipe away the tears from all the people's faces. There will be no more reason to cry, for suffering will have ceased to exist. Verse 8 clearly states that God "will swallow up death forever." Similar to verse 7, the same word "to swallow" is used to describe God's action concerning the most feared enemy, Mot, which broadly can be translated as "death." Hans Wildberger clarifies this term, "*Mot* is anything that causes trouble during one's life, is that which limits the way in which one lives life, is that which takes something away from one's prosperity and gets in the way of fellowship with other humans or with God."[15]

There is an ironic play on words in this text. Ordinarily, the swallowing is done by "the earth" (cf., e.g., Exod 15:12; Num 16:32, 34; 26:10; Deut 11:6; Ps 106:17), the "deep" (Pss 69:15; 96:16), or the "underworld"/"Sheol" (Prov 1:12). But now death and mourning, symbolizing all that threatens life, will be swallowed up (or eaten) by God, suggesting that only when this has been accomplished, God's salvation will be completed.

This text makes the strong statement that God will destroy the last enemy, that is, death, forever. Isaiah 26:19 says something similar when it states that Israel's dead shall live again, that their corpses shall rise from their deathly sleep and start singing for joy. This triumph of life over the forces of death is also seen in the vision of the dry bones coming back to life in Ezek 37. Texts such as these do not directly refer to the resurrection, although later New Testament texts (e.g., 1 Cor 15) would develop accordingly. Rather, these texts talk about a God who completely restores Israel's existence, exhibiting a profound commitment to life.[16] It is significant that this life is imaged in terms of God who abundantly feeds all people at an ongoing feast, where everybody will have enough to eat from the best foods available. The close connection between food and life that is seen throughout this book comes to a climactic finale when Isa 25 portrays God who gives food as also giving life. In this discussion about the end times, life with God is envisioned in terms of a never-ending reality.

DINING THROUGH THE AGES

The idea of an eschatological banquet where God will be victorious over everything that threatens one's peace, where everybody will be able to feast on a sumptuous dinner, truly captured people's attention, so much so that later postbiblical texts did not want to let go of this idea. Accordingly, one sees in many Jewish and Christian texts manifestations of this metaphor of God hosting a glorious banquet that is often linked to a messianic expectation.[17] All of these texts build on the picture created by Isa 25, demonstrating the same emphasis on luxury foods and joyous celebration, which follows God's judgment and removal of the threat of enemies. But in some of these texts, abundance becomes even more superfluous. So one reads in *2 Bar.* 29:5-7 the following description of God's provision of food in the end times, where the banquet not only marks the beginning of the eschatological age, but is a feature of it into perpetuity:

> The earth will also yield fruits ten thousandfold. And on one vine will be a thousand branches, and one branch will produce a thousand clusters, and one cluster will produce a thousand grapes, and one grape will produce a cor [about 364 liters] of wine. And those who are hungry will enjoy themselves and they will, moreover, see marvels every day. For winds will go out in front of me every morning to bring the fragrance of aromatic fruits and clouds at the end of the day to distill the dew of health.[18]

Rabbinic interpreters imagined the abundance of God's provision of food in the end times in an even more elaborate fashion. For instance in *b. Ketub. 111b*, one reads how the wheat will grow as high as a palm tree and how its grain will be as large as the two kidneys of a big bull. When the wheat ripens, the wind will rub the grains together, milling fine flour that can be collected and be sufficient for an entire household.[19] *Sifre Deut.* 316 continues this portrayal by saying that in this time, "a man will bring one grape on a wagon or a ship, put it in a corner of his house and use its contents as if it had been a large wine cask."[20]

Another feature that comes to light in the postbiblical interpretations of the eschatological banquet is that these texts imagine God to provide other sources of miraculous food. *Second Baruch* 29:8 says that in the last days, "the treasury of manna will come down again from on high, and they will eat of it in those years."[21] Thus, God will once again feed people by means of manna, which was considered in chapter 1 as the ultimate symbol of God's provision of food. By using this symbol to envision God's restoration, the metaphor of God's provision of food has gone full circle.

Continuing the theme of victory over all that threatens order and well-being, *2 Bar.* 29:5 states that God will defeat the sea monsters Behemoth and Leviathan, the ultimate symbols of chaos, and use their corpses as food (a lot of food) to feed the faithful in the last days (see also *4 Ezra* 6:52; *1 En.* 60:24).[22] This ironic reference seems to indicate that those things that were most fearsome to Israel will have a useful purpose in the end times.

The New Testament writings build on these traditions of the eschatological banquet when texts, like Luke 13:29 (Matt 8:11), state that people from all the corners of the earth will come to eat at the banquet, which is used to envision the kingdom of God (see also Luke 22:30 where the disciples will eat and drink with Jesus in the kingdom of God). Dennis Smith notes that Luke's Gospel finds the theme of the messianic, or eschatological, banquet well established so that no explanation is needed to clarify its occurrence. Luke uses this metaphor in his own theological project, giving it unique interpretations and accents.[23] This treatment of the New Testament trajectories of the metaphor of God's provision of food is not intended to exhaust the multilayered dimensions of these rich texts. However, this study on the metaphor of the God who feeds may benefit from highlighting a few interpretive tendencies. A number of postbiblical as well as the New Testament appropriations of this metaphor provide some interesting perspectives on the question that was raised earlier in this chapter, namely, who is included in the "all" that is invited to the banquet? Who shares in the communal meal?

Kenneth Bailey shows how a text like *1 En.* 62:1-16 (Isaac) excludes the Gentiles ("the kings and the mighty and the exalted and those who rule the earth"), who will fall down before the Son of Man but will be driven from his presence to a violent death (see also *Tg. Isa.* 25:6 [Chilton]). Also in the Qumran community, where the great banquet is clearly linked with the coming of the Messiah, only the elect of Israel will be included in the meal. The Gentiles and those Jews who have some kind of ailment—who are paralyzed, blind, deaf, or have some skin disease—are excluded (1QSa 2:11-22 [Gaster]). Bailey is of the opinion that "Isaiah's open-ended vision has been blurred, if not eliminated" by these texts.[24]

In the parable of the great banquet in Luke 14:15-24, one sees a radical reversal of these above-mentioned texts, reclaiming something of the universal aspect of Isaiah's message. The parable forms part of a conversation in which Jesus urges his host (a Pharisee) to invite the poor, the disabled, and the blind when he gives a banquet (Luke 14:12-13). One of the table guests answers with the words: "Blessed is anyone who will eat bread in the kingdom of God!" (14:15). Jesus' response to this remark, which relates to the broader question of who would be present at the heavenly banquet, consists of the story of a man whose invitations to his banquet are turned down by his friends, who are too preoccupied with their earthly concerns. He then directs his servant to invite the outsiders of society: the poor, the disabled, and the blind. When there is still more room, the host sends his servants to the highways to bring in people beyond the host's community to fill God's house.

Bailey argues that the eschatological (or messianic) banquet, which was promised in Isa 25:6-9, is "inaugurated in the table fellowship of Jesus."[25] In this regard, Jesus' eating habits are significant. Jesus frequently eats with people who are considered by society as sinners and outcasts (Luke 5:29-32; 15:1-2; 19:5-7). By eating with these people, Jesus is turning the world upside down by including those who are excluded—to echo the words of the Magnificat, "[He has] lifted up the lowly" (Luke 1:52). In the parable of the Great Banquet, it is exactly these outcasts who may come from within or without the community, who are invited to the feast.[26] Moreover, the all-inclusive nature of the banquet in Isa 25 is realized in the parable in Luke 14, when the invitations to the banquet go out beyond the city. We see in this text evidence of the emerging understanding that the Gentiles ought to be included in the "all" who look to God for food.

From these diverse texts from a wide variety of times and places, we see how the metaphor of God's provision of food becomes a striking means of not only expressing God's future restoration but also imagining a future life with God where the final victory over chaos will be achieved. The multiple occurrences of this dimension of God's provision of food and the vibrancy of its expressions attest to the power this metaphor had for people. In the next section, we will reflect on the rhetorical effect that these eschatological visions of the God who will feed again can have for people who live in today's world where more than 800 million people experience hunger.

THE POWER OF IMAGINING A DIFFERENT WORLD

To imagine God as abundantly providing food and hosting a festive banquet where there is enough food for everyone underscores the fact that God wants a good life for all people, a life that is characterized by peace, wholeness, and opportunities for all. The God who feeds indeed wishes people everywhere to have enough food to eat, and one could add, "clothing, shelter, and opportunity for a meaningful existence."[27] However, as we have seen in chapters 2 and 3 of this book, famine is a tragic part of our world today in which multitudes of people are deprived of basic sustenance, not to mention satisfying food that brings pleasure and joy to life.

The images of restoration that have been featured in this chapter all agree that there will be an end to famine. They imagine a glorious future where the natural world is also restored and where everybody will share in the abundance of food that God shall provide. Famine is not part of God's intention for this world. This implies that famine should be fought with the hope that, at the end of time, it will be completely overcome.

It is important to remember that a central theme of this dimension of the metaphor of the God who feeds is that God's provision of food extends to *all* people. In light of this all-inclusive nature of God's provision of food, one can safely say that God wants *all* people everywhere to experience the quality of life that is envisioned in these eschatological visions. However, there is an "already" and "not yet" character to these visions. Although there are instances where God's provision of food is realized in the lives of people who suffer lack—a good example being the acts of compassion that were highlighted in chapter 3 as ways of resisting famine—the food scarcity all around us is a grim reminder that God's banquet has not yet fully commenced. Nevertheless, even though the kingdom of God is expected to become fully realized in the future, the picture it creates has power in the present. These eschatological expressions of God's abundant provision of food are thus "not only announcements of how it will be one day; they are also pronouncements of how it ought to be today."[28]

These visions are thus intended to give hope to those who are in the deepest need. These visions may help people who suffer to look beyond their circumstances, believing that God *is* able to make all things right, creating a future where there will be no more suffering, no more famine. However, this belief is not an excuse for us to sit back and wait for God to do the work. Ethical obligations are embedded in these eschatological promises. The visions or images of God's future kingdom motivate us toward active engagement with God to bring the present state of things into conformity with our vision of how God intended life to be. As Dempsey puts it: "we roll up our sleeves and get to work."[29] Thus, to share our bread, and to fight against injustice, poverty, and illness is to actualize something of God's heavenly banquet today.

On the other hand, we know all too well that people's best efforts are limited and that the challenges are overbearing. When people find themselves in a situation of despair about the futility of their efforts, we can find comfort in the fact that, in the end, the future is in God's hands. As Gowan argues, "Whether we succeed or fail, our every effort to make things right is, therefore, a witness to the world that God is at work to bring about, someday, a time without suffering and anguish for everyone. Every little victory over evil is thus a reminder that the ultimate victory is coming."[30]

It thus seems as if these eschatological visions exhibit a dual effect. For people who are complacent, focusing on the status quo, saying that one day things will be different, the metaphor of God who abundantly feeds God's children challenges them to help create a society in the here and now that mirrors this divine claim. And for those people who feel helpless, who feel overwhelmed by reality, it may be comforting to look forward to a time when God will host a banquet where there will be no more hunger or suffering.

HOSTING A BANQUET FOR HER CHILDREN

In what way can these visions that describe God's restoration of Israel in terms of God's provision of food be used to reimagine the metaphor of God's provision of food in female terms? In fact, there is nothing inherently female in the eschatological visions that have been introduced in this chapter. However, there is one more restoration text that could change the way we think about this dimension of the metaphor of the God who feeds. In Isa 66:11-13, one finds an image of a mother nursing her child, which is used to describe God's restoration of Israel. Reading this text in conjunction with other restoration texts that portray God's abundant provision of food may bestow some female associations on the metaphor of the God who feeds.

The metaphor of nursing in Isa 66:11-13 appears right after a metaphor of childbirth that is used in Isa 66:7-10 to describe the rebirth of the people. In verse 8, we see that the mother who gives birth without even having any labor pains is the city Zion, Jerusalem, who has brought forth the restored nation. But whereas Mother Zion was mourning the loss of her children (see ch. 3), everybody will now rejoice and be glad for her (v. 10) because she has given birth to the restored nation of Israel. The unique metaphor of the miraculous birth of the people in Isa 66 vividly expresses the hope that is also present in other restoration texts—a new life lies ahead; a new age has arrived.

In verse 9, we discover God's role in this birthing process. God emphasizes by means of a rhetorical question, as well as the emphatic use of the pronoun "I," that it indeed is God who opens the womb (הַאֲנִי אַשְׁבִּיר) and delivers (אוֹלִיד) the child. God, the One who is called "the deliverer" or "midwife" (הַמּוֹלִיד), is the One who has restored Israel's fortunes.

Now that the baby is born, we see in verse 11 how Zion tends to her newborn, how the people nurse (תִּינְקוּ) from her consoling breast and are totally satisfied. In this text, an image of nursing is used to express something of the new life that the newly created people's lives will experience. Elsewhere, this restoration was imaged in terms of renewed food supplies based on the understanding that God once more provided food in abundance after the excruciating times of famine. In Isa 66:11-13, the people will also eat and have enough, but this time, the metaphor fits the status of a newborn who nurses from the ample milk that her mother Zion provides. The food that they receive from their mother is truly life-giving, heralding the new life they are experiencing.

In verse 12 it becomes clear who is responsible for the people being able to "drink deeply with delight from [Zion's] glorious bosom" (v. 11). Verse 12 states that it is *God* who extends peace and well-being to Zion. Moreover, it is God who causes the riches of the other nations to flow like a river back into Jerusalem. One could thus argue that it is God who makes it possible for the people to "nurse" on the food that God once more has provided to God's children. One could even say that God feeds or "nurses" God's children by means of Mother Zion.

We see this direct correlation between God and Israel's restored fortunes in two instances. In verse 12*b*, a direct consequence of God's actions will be that the people shall nurse, be carried on Zion's arm, and be bounced on her knees. God's role is even more evident in verse 13 when the image switches from Zion being the mother who takes care of the people to God as the divine Mother who comforts her children.[31] A threefold repetition of the term *to comfort* emphasizes God's amazing maternal love.[32] God emphatically affirms that Godself will comfort the people. Once more, God and Jerusalem "mother" together as verse 13*b* uses the passive tense to repeat that the people shall be comforted (תנחמו) in Jerusalem. These images of comfort create a picture of the city and God working together to tenderly raise their precious child.

The striking maternal metaphor that is used to describe God's restoration of Israel encourages us to think differently about the other texts that use the metaphor of the God's renewed provision of food. The metaphor of God who abundantly feeds God's children is gender neutral, thus there is nothing explicitly female about this metaphor. However, in light of the striking nursing imagery that was used in a number of biblical texts as well as in postbiblical interpretations (cf. chs. 1, 4), it could be quite interesting to also imagine God's renewed provision of food in female terms. The female associations introduced by Isa 66, as well as the picture of God hosting a banquet, could be used in the following way to imagine God's provision of food in terms of a hostess who once more hosts a glorious party.

After the longest time, God once more pulls the recipe books off the shelf. This time, she decides to host a wonderful banquet. She takes care to only use the very best ingredients to make the most delicious dishes imaginable. And the wines are carefully chosen to complement the meal. She smiles when she pictures how much her guests will enjoy the festivity. They will all have more than enough to eat, and the sounds of laughter and pleasant conversation will fill the room. All her children will be there around the table—every last one of them. She will make sure that those children who have special needs will be close to her side so that she can make sure they are taken care of. And where they once quarreled outside the house about the trivialities with which children often occupy themselves, the mood at her banquet will be one of joy and well-being. This meal will be as satisfying as those days when she carried her child against her breast, resting peacefully after having nursed to his or her heart's delight.

There will be no more sadness at her feast. Her children will forget all the tears they cried during their earthly lives. There will be no more hunger, no more illness, and most certainly no more death. She will make sure of that. At her table, there will be only room for joyous community. And this meal that she will host will endure forever.

CHAPTER 5

"COME, EAT OF MY BREAD AND DRINK OF THE WINE I HAVE MIXED"

The Relation of Woman Wisdom as Nourisher to the God Who Feeds

One final dimension of the metaphor of the God who feeds concerns its presence in the wisdom traditions. Before focusing on the unique perspectives associated with this dimension of God's provision of food, I have a few words about how wisdom fits into this project as a whole. The place of wisdom in biblical theology is an issue of much contention. Scholars have struggled to find ways of incorporating wisdom into an Old Testament or a biblical theology. Claus Westermann has even stated outright that wisdom has no place within a formal Old Testament theology, but that it should be appropriated in the context of human creation.[1] Even to put wisdom at the end of this book may suggest that it is no more than a mere afterthought. However, in my mind, wisdom is an exceedingly important aspect of any biblical or Old Testament theology. Although the wisdom material is placed last in this book, it is done with the assumption that wisdom is "at play" in every phase of Israel's continuing reflection on the metaphor of the God who feeds.[2]

Particularly the model for a biblical theology that I proposed in the introduction resolves some of the difficulty of incorporating wisdom. The notion of dialogue, which forms the structuring concept for this project, implies that meaning is not to be found in any one of the individual chapters but within the space where the diverse voices interact. This means that if one regards these texts together, one could well imagine wisdom at work in all of the different dimensions of the metaphor of the God who feeds.

This is true of every facet of Israel's reflection on the God who feeds: from Israel's basic expression concerning God's provision of food as an integral part of creation to the times of suffering, lack, and disorientation during which people perceived God as failing to feed and to a renewed ability to integrate past experiences and move toward a new orientation regarding God and life's challenges and joys. In each of these dimensions, people reflected on life's existential questions in relation to God's provision of food, using some of the same skills inherent to the wisdom traditions. And when Israel had to imagine how a life of learning and teaching should look, their belief that God is the God who feeds once more influenced the way in which they construed a life searching for God. Accordingly, we will see in this chapter how the wisdom traditions once more creatively used the multifaceted metaphor of God providing food, which not only provides vital perspectives on the metaphor of God's provision of food but also offers some of the boldest expressions of the female dimension of God.

This is particularly evident in the way the intriguing character of Woman Wisdom relates to the metaphor of the God who feeds. In a number of biblical and postbiblical traditions, we encounter the image of Wisdom who provides food. This portrayal forms part of a comprehensive personification of Wisdom as a woman who manifests herself in various roles as mother, lover, teacher, herald, and also as host.[3] We will see in this chapter how food serves as a symbol of learning that is encapsulated in the figure of Woman Wisdom providing food.

Several helpful studies have been done on the topic of Wisdom who provides food, most significantly the works by Karl-Gustav Sandelin, *Wisdom as Nourisher,* and Judith E. McKinlay, *Gendering Wisdom the Host.*[4] These two works feature prominently in this exposition. Moreover, there is a profusion of studies that wrestle with the complex questions surrounding the identity of Woman Wisdom and her relationship with God.[5] Without rehashing all the arguments in a debate that has not brought anywhere near a clear consensus, this chapter focuses narrowly on the question of how Woman Wisdom's provision of food relates to the metaphor of the God who feeds.

WHEN WISDOM PROVIDES FOOD

In Prov 9:1-6 we encounter Woman Wisdom where she is busy preparing a lavish banquet to which she will invite people to come share in her gifts of food and drink. The first thing we read is that Wisdom is building her house. The house exhibits powerful associations of stability and permanence (cf. 2 Sam 7:13, 16, 27)—the seven pillars signifying completeness or perfection. In addition, the multipillared house serves as an indication of prosperity and affluence (Prov 24:3-4). Overall, Prov 9 images Wisdom as creating the perfect and long-lasting mansion with room for many guests—the ideal setting in which to host her banquet.

Woman Wisdom's invitation to the meal is preceded by extensive preparations for the banquet. She herself slaughters her meat for the festival (lit., "slaughter her slaughterings" טבחה טבחה), mixes her wine, and sets her table. The repetition of the personal pronoun in these verses emphasizes that these gifts are hers to give. The food provided is not simply the basic food provisions of bread and water but a lavish, expensive meal. She offers meat that would have been considered a luxury item, accompanied by wine mixed with spices, which denotes the intoxicating drink enjoyed at a feast (Prov 23:30; Isa 5:22).

After her careful preparations, Woman Wisdom sends out her servants—a detail that attests to her position of status in society—to go invite her guests to the banquet. There is a sense of urgency to her invitation, emphasized by the three imperatives, "come," "eat," and "drink." Wisdom promises that if the guests dine on the meal that she has prepared and the wine that she has mixed, they will receive the gift of life.[6] In verse 6 we see how "to live" means to "walk in the way of insight." This reference continues the connections between learning and food and life that we have seen in chapter 1 (e.g., Deut 8:3). In the same way that food is considered to be necessary to sustain life, so does the word or wisdom or knowledge give life. Michael Fox recognizes this connection when he states that "to listen to Wisdom, to live within her house, to partake of her food and wine, are different ways to envision a lifetime of learning."[7] A "lifetime of learning" thus equals life. What better way to express this notion than by the life-giving symbol of food that our bodies need daily to stay healthy and alive? But in this text, Wisdom is providing not only basic sustenance but also the richest foods that symbolize the splendor that a "lifetime of learning" can offer.

Important to note is the connection between Wisdom's gift of food and God that this text assumes. Just as Wisdom promises life (Prov 9:6), so a number of texts in Proverbs maintain that the fear of the Lord leads to life (Prov 10:27; 14:27; 19:23; 22:4). Indeed, wisdom begins and ends with the fear or reverence of God (Prov 1:7; 9:10). Or as Prov 2:6 states: "For God gives wisdom; from God's mouth come knowledge and understanding" (AT). In essence, Wisdom not only presents with her gifts of food the content of wisdom but also points to the Giver of wisdom. To partake from the food that Wisdom offers is to choose life with God.

WISDOM'S PROVISION OF FOOD AND THE GOD WHO FEEDS

In reference to the image of Woman Wisdom's act of building a house and hosting a banquet in Prov 9:1-6, Judith McKinlay argues that scholars have sought to understand this image by placing her into a particular interpretative framework. Based on various ancient Near Eastern parallels, Woman Wisdom is for instance read in terms of a cosmological setting where her house metaphorically suggests the creation of the world, or a cultic background where she is regarded as the goddess Wisdom, who after having built her temple, sends out priestesses to invite people to come and worship her.[8]

McKinlay notes that each of these frameworks "provides a different lens through which to view this female figure," which will obviously influence the way we can understand Woman Wisdom. Without denying the validity of these interpretations, McKinlay offers another possible interpretative framework in which to read the figure of Wisdom as Host. In light of the fact that Woman Wisdom is offering nothing less than the gifts of God, McKinlay suggests that it may be quite rewarding to read Woman Wisdom's gifts of food in terms of the God who feeds.[9] In light of the portrayal of God as the Gracious Provider of food, I argue that to follow McKinlay's suggestion yields some valuable insight on the question at the heart of this chapter: How does Woman Wisdom's provision of food relate to the metaphor of the God who feeds? In the previous chapters, I showed how God's gifts of food lead to life and how connections with teaching and learning surfaced in connection with God's provision of food. In light of the similar connections that were highlighted in Woman Wisdom's depiction in Prov 9, it seems plausible that Wisdom's act of providing food parallels that of the God who feeds. We will see in a number of biblical and postbiblical texts how this relationship manifests itself.

One text that forms part of McKinlay's proposed interpretative framework is Isa 55. Several scholars have shown similarities between the form and content of Isa 55 and Prov 9.[10] In Isa 55:1-2, the speaker urgently invites his or her audience in a threefold repetition of the imperative "to come." They are invited to "come," "buy," and "eat" from the sumptuous gifts of food he is offering: the wine and the rich milk well-suited for the festival. The remarkable thing about this invitation is that it is free. People are encouraged to come buy the expensive fare without money.

This appealing invitation encourages the audience to make the good news of the return from exile their own. The invitation suggests something of the "inner appropriation" of the "total self" (see also Ezek 2:8–3:3).[11] The audience is called to take part in the feast, to eat what is good, and to delight themselves in rich food. To "come," "buy," "eat," "listen," and "delight" all suggest actions of participation. Like food and drink become part of the body, so the word and the prophet's message should be fully embraced.

Important to note is that *God* is the One who is offering the invitation (see particularly v. 3*b*). As we have seen in so many places in the Old Testament and postbiblical texts, God feeds God's children with God's bountiful gifts of food and wine. In Isa 55, the promise of returning home from exile is imaged once more in terms of the metaphor of God's provision of food. Good food, rich food, is to be found with God alone. And what's more, to dine on God's gifts of food, to listen, and to make the message their own is to receive the gift of life (v. 3; see also vv. 6-7).

The food that God offers not only is appetizing and life-giving but also brings *joy*. We have seen in Ps 104:15 how God has given wine to gladden people's hearts. This emphasis on joy is also evident in the ending of Isa 55, where all the mountains and the hills will break out in song, and the trees of the field will clap their hands when the exiles return in joy (vv. 12-13). The joyous message of God's invitation is that God's word will not return empty but will accomplish what God has promised. God's word will be like the rain that waters the earth, which will cause the earth to sprout seeds, leading to seed for the sower and bread for the eater (vv. 10-11). This is indeed reason for celebration as suggested by the festival with rich food offerings that is used to describe this invitation.

Isaiah 55 introduces another connection to describe God's gift of life when verses 3-4 take the promise to David and interpret it in a strikingly new fashion. Now, the everlasting promise to David, which serves as the epitome of God's steadfast love and grace (2 Sam 7; Ps 89), will be extended to all people. God's covenant with David now functions as a symbol of the new life given by God. One could say that "the house" that God had promised to build for David in 2 Sam 7:11, which denoted a sense of permanence and stability, now is opened to all people who would heed the invitation and join the festival that leads to life.

When read together, it becomes clear that the invitation to join the festival and live in Isa 55 looks very much like Woman Wisdom's invitation in Prov 9, where the participation in her gifts of food also leads to life. Both texts use gifts of food to invite their respective audiences to enter into a life with God. In both texts, food is employed as a symbol for God's word, which needs to be embraced by the hearers. One receives this gift of life by loving God, walking in God's ways, and keeping God's commandments. Isaiah 55 clearly says that God is the One offering the invitation in words that sound very much like that of Woman Wisdom in Prov 9. Since what Woman Wisdom is really offering in Prov 9 is a life with God, it seems that her gifts of food parallel that of God's provision of food in Isa 55. Subsequently, McKinlay says about Woman Wisdom in Prov 9, "Read with this understanding, Wisdom, in whatever guise, is implicitly the Wisdom of Yahweh."[12] When Woman Wisdom is providing food, she really is evoking the God who feeds.

The following rabbinic interpretation also links Wisdom's provision of food in parallel fashion with the God who feeds. Rabbi Jeremiah b. Ila'i expounds the image of Wisdom hosting a banquet in Prov 9:1-4 as referring to the creation of the world in *Lev. Rab.* 11:1. (Italics represent a quotation within a quotation.) He says,

> "*Wisdom hath builded her house*" refers to the Holy One, blessed be He, as it is said, *The Lord by wisdom founded the earth* (Prov. III, 19). "*She hath hewn out her seven pillars*" refers to the seven days at the Beginning, as it is said, *For in six days the Lord made heaven and earth, the sea, and all that in them is, and rested on the seventh day* (Ex. XX, 11), also, *And God blessed the seventh day* (Gen. II, 3). "*She hath prepared her object of slaughtering*" is an allusion to, *And God said: Let the earth bring forth the living*

creature after its kind, cattle, etc. (*ib*. I, 24). *"She hath mingled her wine"* is an allusion to, *And God said: Let the waters . . . be gathered together, etc.* (*ib*. 9), *"She hath also furnished her table"* is an allusion to, *And God said: Let the earth put forth grass* (*ib*. 11). *"She hath sent forth . . . she calleth her servants,"* alluding to Adam and Eve.[13]

It seems that to think of Wisdom's provision of food in terms of God as Provider is nothing new. This midrash makes a clever connection between Wisdom's act of providing food and God's provision of food. In creative fashion, this midrash draws a parallel between Wisdom who first builds her house, prepares the food, and then calls out to the servants, and God, who, as we have seen in chapter 2, in creation first prepared a home with food aplenty before creating humans.

Something of this understanding is found in Raymond van Leeuwen's interpretation of Prov 9. He sees a parallel between God's act of building the cosmos in Prov 8:22-29 and Wisdom building her house in Prov 9:1-6. He cites two texts from Proverbs to illustrate this parallel: First, according to Prov 3:19-20, God founded the earth (יסד־ארץ) by means of wisdom (בחכמה) and established (כונן) the heavens by means of understanding (בתבונה). Second, in Prov 24:3, one finds a parallel text that says by means of wisdom (בחכמה) a house is built (יבנה בית), and by means of understanding it is established (ובתבונה יתכונן). According to Van Leeuwen, in these two passages, "house building is parallel to cosmos building."[14]

Similar to the midrash in *Lev. Rab.* 11, Wisdom's act of building a house evokes God's building of the cosmos. This statement raises the very complex issue of how to understand Wisdom's role in creation. The text in Prov 8:22-31 that deals with Wisdom's origins and role in creation lends itself to diverse interpretations, primarily stemming from the ambiguous nature of the text itself.[15] One sees this most clearly illustrated in the sharp divisions among the earliest interpretations of the text as manifested in the various textual variants. There is no consensus on the many interpretative options. Whether one regards Wisdom's role in creation as that of an active participant (a "master craftsperson" or "architect") or a little child whose sole function is to delight God, at the very least it can be said that her involvement and presence at the time of creation suggests a special relationship with God.[16] Furthermore, the text leaves open the possibility that Wisdom may be a way to talk about God's creative activity. For instance, later texts pick up the interpretation that Wisdom is a kind of architect in creation; Wis 7:21 calls her "the fashioner of all things" (ἡ γὰρ πάντων τεχνῖτις). And *Gen. Rab.* 1:1

reflects this tradition when it says that God consulted the Torah when creating the world (Torah being equated with Wisdom in Ben Sirach).[17] Accordingly, this more active role of Woman Wisdom in creation could conceivably be understood as God creating by means of Wisdom.

An analogous argument could be made concerning Wisdom's provision of food, arguing for a link between Wisdom's gifts of food and those of the God who feeds. As Van Leeuwen proposes,

> The food and drink prepared by Lady Wisdom are metaphors for the life-giving gifts of creation (9:6). Her "house" is full, and she offers, in effect, to fill the "house" of her guests.... To enter Wisdom's house is to enter the life-giving center of the cosmos, a Garden of Eden where creation's goods are most intensely present and accessible.... In Wisdom's house all the goods of creation are to be found, for God made them all "by wisdom" (cf. Ps 104:24).[18]

Once more there is a parallel between Wisdom's and God's provision of food. One could say that Wisdom's gift of food symbolizes something of the God who feeds the world with God's abundant gifts of food. Or that Woman Wisdom's provision of food evokes the God who feeds God's children.

TRACING THE RELATIONSHIP IN POSTBIBLICAL LITERATURE

The close association between Woman Wisdom as nourisher and the God who feeds that we have seen thus far continues in the vibrant literature of the postbiblical period. For instance, in Sir 15:2-3, Wisdom is likened to a mother and a young bride who offers the one who fears God, keeps the law, and seeks wisdom her gifts of food and drink. Verse 3 says that "she will feed him with the bread of learning, / and give him the water of wisdom to drink."

This text uses two female images to describe Woman Wisdom in her capacity as nourisher. The use of mothering imagery may be related to the tendency of later postbiblical texts to use nursing language as an illustration of learning (cf. ch. 1). In addition, the image of a young bride may evoke connotations of sexual imagery that is used in some wisdom texts in reference to learning.[19]

The appearance of Woman Wisdom in Sir 15 relates to two texts that were seen earlier in this chapter, that is, Prov 9 and Isa 55. Sandelin argues that all of these texts build on the Old Testament understanding of God providing bread, namely the paradigmatic story of the manna in wilderness. Thus, Sandelin believes that Wisdom acts here in a way similar to God in the Old Testament. He concludes that "the bread and water that Wisdom gives are in reality bread and water from God."[20] In addition, Sandelin sees a correspondence between Sirach's depiction of Wisdom as mother in Sir 15:2 and the portrayal of God as the ultimate Mother, who will not forget Israel in Isa 49:14. Once more, there is a similarity between the way God and Wisdom are portrayed.

A second text in the book of Sirach that uses Woman Wisdom's gifts of food as a metaphor to describe the act of learning is Sir 24:12-21. This text compares her to a multitude of trees (cf. the initial identification with the tree of life in Prov 3:18), including the vine that yields an abundance of fruit. In verse 19, Wisdom invites her audience to come eat of these fruits. To possess her is sweeter than a honeycomb. And in verse 21, she says that those who eat of her will hunger for more and those who drink of her will thirst for more.

Verse 23 identifies the fruits of Woman Wisdom that generate this unquenchable thirst and hunger as the law of Moses—once more developing the connection between food, learning, and life. Learning is equated to delicious fruit that serves the function to sustain life, similar to the waters of the rivers that are mentioned in verses 25-31. But these fruits are also sweet to the taste and symbolize the fact that the act of learning, that is, to make the teaching and the way of Wisdom (God) one's own is to be a joyous occasion.

By means of inviting people to partake from the fruits she offers, Woman Wisdom encourages people to participate in a life with God. A food metaphor best illustrates this engagement with the Torah. Thus by eating and drinking the gifts of food that Wisdom offers, one truly embraces the word, wisdom, or the law as one's own. In following the law, one encounters not only Wisdom but also God. Wisdom thus functions as a way to God, who manifests Godself in Wisdom. In this regard, Sandelin further notes that when Ben Sirach alludes to Old Testament texts, he often refers to "Wisdom" where the Old Testament texts have "God" (e.g., Pss 1:2; 37:40). Accordingly, "the teaching and way of God" is substituted by "the teaching and the way of Wisdom." Sandelin argues that this does not mean that Wisdom has taken God's place but that, for

Sirach, "the teaching and the way of Wisdom is in fact nothing but the teaching and the way of the Lord."[21]

One sees in these texts from Sirach how Wisdom's gifts of food really point to the God who feeds. Thus in the Torah, Wisdom's provision of food evokes God whose word or teaching sustains and gives life to those who embrace a life of learning.

A last text that makes a distinct connection between Wisdom's provision of food and the God who feeds is from Philo's allegorical commentary on Gen 4:8-15, *That the Worse Attacks the Better (Quod deterius potiori insidari soleat)*; *Det.* 115–118 is a good example of Philo's tendency of making intriguing connections between various theological concepts.[22]

These "products" are nourishment [τροφαί] in the strict meaning of the word, supplied [θηλάζειν "suckled"] by the soul that is able, as the lawgiver says, to "suck honey out of the rock [μέλι ἐκ πέτρας] and oil out of the hard rock" [ἔλαιον ἐκ στερεᾶς πέτρας] (ibid. [Deut 32:13]). [Moses] uses the word "rock" [πέτραν] to express the solid and indestructible wisdom of God [σοφίαν θεοῦ], which feeds [τροφόν] and nurses [τιθηνοκόμον] and rears to sturdiness all who yearn after imperishable sustenance [τῶν ἀφθάρτου διαίτης]. For this divine wisdom has appeared as mother of all that are in the world [μήτηρ τῶν ἐν κόσμῳ], affording to her offspring, as soon as they are born, the nourishment [τὰς τροφάς] which they require from her own breasts. But not all her offspring are [worthy to eat] divine food [τροφῆς θείας], but such as are found worthy of their parents; for many of them fall victims to the famine of virtue, a famine more cruel than that of eatables and drinkables. The fountain of the divine wisdom [τῆς θείας σοφίας] runs sometimes with a gentler and more quiet stream, at other times more swiftly and with a fuller and stronger current. When it runs down gently, it sweetens much as honey [μέλιτος] does; when it runs swiftly down, it comes in full volume as material for lighting up the soul, even as oil [ἔλαιον] does a lamp. In another place he uses a synonym for this rock [τὴν πέτραν] and calls it "manna" [μάννα]. Manna is the divine word [λόγον θεῖον], eldest of all existences, which bears the most comprehensive name of "Somewhat."[23] Out of it are made two cakes [δύο ἐγκρίδες], the one of honey [μέλιτος], the other of oil [ἔλαίου]. These are two inseparable and all-important stages in education, at the outset causing a sweetness to flow from what knowledge opens, and afterwards causing a most brilliant light to flash from them on those who handle in no fickle and perfunctory way the subjects which they love, but lay hold of them strongly and firmly with a persistence that knows no slackness or intermission.[24]

In an exposition of the word for "products" (γεννήματα) in Philo's version of Gen 4:12, Philo develops the allegorical meaning when he says that these products are virtues, which are nourishment for the soul. The soul receives this nourishment by means of nursing. The reference to nursing introduces the prooftext of Deut 32:13, which says that one suckles honey out of the rock and oil out of the hard rock.

One sees from this exposition how Philo makes a connection in *Det.* 115–118 between the rock and Wisdom. One should keep in mind that in Deut 32:13 God is the One who fed or nursed Israel with honey and oil from the rock. Philo now equates the rock with Wisdom, who is said to be the mother who feeds, nurses, and rears all in the world. She provides everyone with nourishment from her own breasts. Thus, as God fed Israel with honey and oil from the rock, so God feeds people with knowledge by means of Wisdom. The divine nutrition flows like a stream from Wisdom's breasts. There are different levels involved in the transmission of knowledge. The first stage is said to be the initial level of opening up knowledge, where the stream of knowledge flows gently as it sweetens like honey. The second stage is signified by oil, which flows with a quicker stream, which, as Philo says, causes "a most brilliant light to flash," and which "grips its subjects firmly." Philo links these two stages with the two cakes made from manna—the one of oil and the other of honey.[25]

It is significant to see that Philo makes a connection between Wisdom, who nurses her children, and manna, which stands for the divine word. *Deterius* 115–118 thus uses an image of nursing to describe the manna that was considered to be the essential symbol of God's provision in the wilderness. However, in this text, Philo makes a further connection between God's provision of food and Woman Wisdom as nourisher, thereby bestowing distinctive female associations on the metaphor of the God who feeds. Philo says that nutrition, that is, teaching, comes from Wisdom's own breasts, providing a further illustration of manna and nursing imagery being used in reference to learning or teaching. Wisdom as nourisher now comes to signify Wisdom as teacher. And her teaching activity is expressed by means of the metaphor of a mother nursing.

Once more, we see in this text a close association between Wisdom as nourisher and the God who feeds. Philo asserts in *Det.* 115–118 that *Wisdom* is the one feeding her children, thereby performing an equivalent function to God, who ordinarily is the giver of manna. God satisfies souls with Wisdom and, through her nourishment, provides for people's souls.

One could argue that *Det.* 115–118 formulates the relationship between Woman Wisdom and the God who feeds as follows: if God provides the nourishment for the souls through Wisdom and if God is thought to be the giver of manna, then God nurses her children with heavenly food.

This parallel or equivalent relationship between Wisdom's provision of food and the God who feeds is something that we have seen in other biblical and postbiblical texts discussed earlier. In addition, in all of these texts, we have in greater or lesser fashion distinct female associations surrounding Woman Wisdom's gifts of food. In most of these texts, Woman Wisdom's gifts of food evoke the God who feeds. In at least the last text by Philo, this connection is made even more apparent when God is said to feed, or actually nurse, God's children by means of Wisdom.

WOMAN WISDOM AS THE DIVINE PRESENCE

The close relationship between Wisdom as nourisher and the God who feeds relates to the complex discussion of how to explain the relationship between Woman Wisdom (Sophia) and God in biblical and postbiblical wisdom texts. This discussion is important for at least two reasons. First, scholars agree that the relationship between God and Wisdom is significant because it played a central role in the development of Christology.[26] The relationship between Woman Wisdom and God provided important conceptual categories for early Christian writers to express the relationship between Jesus and God. Elizabeth Johnson, following scholars like Raymond Brown and James Dunn, argues that the New Testament writings make such a close identification between Jesus and Sophia regarding their nature and role that Jesus can be described as Sophia herself.[27] More will be said about this development in chapter 6. Second, the relationship between God and the female entity of Woman Wisdom is particularly important for feminist theology as this relationship presents the opportunity to develop the female dimension of God. Scholars like Elizabeth Johnson compellingly argue that Woman Wisdom presents one of the most poignant expressions of the female dimension of God. I will discuss the implications for a feminist Christology in chapter 6.

The relationship between Woman Wisdom and God is multifaceted. One should be careful not to lose sight of this complexity when moving toward some kind of theological systematization. As Roland Murphy rightly points out, Woman Wisdom cannot be captured or "adequately defined" at any one point throughout her journey from Proverbs to the postbiblical books.[28] However, a number of broad interpretative tendencies may offer an angle for understanding something of this intricate relationship. With a full awareness of the complexities involved and realizing that scholars are divided on the details, I will lift up two points for the purpose of this discussion.

First, most scholars show how God and Woman Wisdom are intrinsically related. For instance, a text quoted by all of these scholars to illustrate the peak of the development between God and Woman Wisdom comes from the book of Wisdom of Solomon. In this first-century B.C.E.–first-century C.E. book from Alexandria, the figure of Woman Wisdom (Sophia) and God are depicted in an especially close relation. In Wis 7:25-26, Sophia is

> a breath [ἀτμὶς] of the power of God,
> and a pure emanation [ἀπόρροια] of the glory of the Almighty;
> therefore nothing defiled gains entrance into her.
> For she is a reflection [ἀπαύγασμα] of eternal light,
> a spotless mirror [ἔσοπτρον ἀκηλίδωτον] of the working of God,
> and an image [εἰκὼν] of his goodness.

We find here that Sophia is portrayed as essentially being a part of God. Being a breath of God's power and an emanation of God's glory, one can describe her as originating from God. When one sees Sophia, one sees God, since she reflects, mirrors, and images Godself. On the other hand, one should note that the relationship between Sophia and God is one of both similarity and difference. Although God and Sophia are intrinsically related, they are still distinguishable.

Second, scholars explain this close relationship in the following way. Johnson describes Sophia, in relation to God, as "a personification of God's own self in creative and saving involvement with the world."[29] This is most evident in Wis 10, where the whole of Israel's salvation history is reinterpreted in light of Wisdom's saving power. Here it seems as if Sophia's actions and those of God are virtually the same, that Wisdom is in reality Godself in God's activity in the world.

On the basis of this text as well as the other texts mentioned in this chapter, it appears as if Sophia becomes a necessary means of expressing a transcendent God's immanence to this world. Accordingly, Johnson asserts that Woman Wisdom personifies God and actually is "an expression of the most intense divine presence in the world."[30] Samuel Terrien makes a similar argument in his book *The Elusive Presence,* where he describes Wisdom as the "mediatrix of presence." He argues that Woman Wisdom offered a model for "the paradox" of God's "presence in absence."[31] A slightly different interpretation is given by Roland Murphy, who argues against the notion of Woman Wisdom being an intermediary. According to him, this would make of God "a kind of absentee landlord." Nevertheless, Woman Wisdom brings for him "a sense of divine presence and closeness to all of creation that is simply unequalled." There is accordingly for Murphy an interesting mix of transcendence and immanence encapsulated in the figure of Woman Wisdom.[32] Regardless of the precise definition of Woman Wisdom, all of these scholars agree that she evokes God's presence in the world and in the process becomes a way of talking about God and God's action.

Scholars like Elizabeth Johnson and Martin Scott have used these arguments to construct a case for conceiving of Woman Wisdom as the female dimension of the divine. Johnson formulates this view, "Sophia is in reality God herself in her activity in the world, God imaged as a female acting subject."[33]

Within this formulation, one point should be clarified: various scholars who acknowledge the close association between Woman Wisdom and God, and even see them as equivalent, will still argue that Sophia is the female representation of God's activity in the world without compromising the male Yahweh as the acting agent. In this regard, one has to accept the historical reality that the biblical writers were thoroughly subsumed within a patriarchal framework. This reality leads McKinlay to argue that the female Wisdom imagery is "clearly kept within the boundaries of the one god Yahweh."[34] Accordingly, one should not romanticize the female associations surrounding Woman Wisdom. McKinlay goes to great length showing how postbiblical interpreters like Ben Sirach "mistreat" the literary figure of Woman Wisdom by using her as part of his androcentric framework.[35] And Philo, heavily influenced by Platonism and his views of human sexuality, withdraws Sophia from the upper realm and replaces her work by that of the male Logos. Philo even tries to diminish her sexuality, on one occasion, making her male instead of female.[36]

Nevertheless, McKinlay can still argue that this reality should not prohibit us from celebrating the fact that the "use of a feminine symbol as a way of talking about God and God's gifts to the world was in itself a gift to Israel's religious tradition."[37] If one accepts that the mystery of God implies that God is neither male nor female, but that both male and female metaphors are used to describe God, one could regard Woman Wisdom as a female metaphor that is used to imagine God. Woman Wisdom then functions as a symbol of God in her creating and sustaining activity in the world.

What is needed in this regard is what McKinlay calls reading the text against itself. This entails that one is aware of the complex gender dynamics that are present in these texts. Although they present us with the intrinsic relationship between Woman Wisdom and God, one still needs to critically and sometimes subversively engage in developing the female dimension of the divine.[38] Regardless of the potential difficulties involved, there is something powerful about breaking through the strictly male pictures that have dominated theological discourse for so long. A critical reconstruction that uses the available resources to find new ways of expressing something of the mystery of God could be very powerful indeed.

Particularly regarding the metaphor of the God who feeds, the theological expression that flows from these texts provides us with a rich resource for imagining God's provision of food in female terms. We have seen throughout this chapter numerous female associations that are associated with Woman Wisdom's provision of food. If one accepts the position that Woman Wisdom functions as God in the world, one could argue that these female associations color the metaphor of the God who feeds in the following way.

Woman Wisdom, as the most intense expression of the God who feeds, bestows her gifts of food to all of her children. She invites them to participate in a lifelong activity of learning, which is envisioned as the most intimate communion with her. Her children are invited to dwell in her house, which suggests a long-term arrangement, denoting a sense of permanence and stability. In Sirach, this learning is typified in terms of Wisdom's identification with the Torah, inviting students (mostly male in that time, but we can and should think of the student body in inclusive terms) to meet her in the study of God's Torah.

God offers her students bread and water, the basic foods necessary for life—hearkening back to the time in the wilderness where they only had God's gifts of manna and water from the rock to depend on for survival. These gifts of food express the necessity of learning to nourish the soul—something that is as necessary for life as bread and water. To eat and drink from her gifts is to participate fully in the life with God, symbolizing complete communion with the Giver.

But God's gifts of learning do not just comprise the bare minimum to sustain life. God does not want her children only to survive, but to thrive. There is a sense of abundance associated with God's gifts of food. Learning, life, and communion with God is imaged as a lavish feast with rich foods and wine. This depicts something of the joy that God wants her children to experience in the act of learning, which does not stand loose from life but in its very center.

CHAPTER 6

GOD'S PROVISION OF FOOD IN THE NEW TESTAMENT AND BEYOND

So far, we have seen some powerful expressions of the metaphor of the God who feeds. We encountered the metaphor of God's provision of food in the contrasting depictions of superfluity and starvation, of life and death. We saw beautiful depictions of people's deepest confidence in the God who feeds. However, in times of lack, we also saw how the only logical conclusion people could reach was that God was withholding food. How do we make sense of these contrasting perspectives?

According to the model for biblical theology that formed the basis of this book, meaning is not to be found in any one of the divergent dimensions of the metaphor of the God who feeds, but in the midst of the space where these dimensions interact. In light of the fact that the different voices within the dialogue are not collapsed, each dimension adds an important perspective to the metaphor of the God who feeds. For this reason, it is essential to remember the painful memories depicted in the biblical traditions and not to jump too quickly to the words of hope of a God who will feed again. To do this would cheapen the reality of believers' experience of pain and hurt. But at the same time, we also know that suffering never speaks the last word in the biblical text. The powerful affirmation that God will feed again is testimony to this understanding. To keep the visions of pain and healing in tension makes for an honest and comprehensive depiction of the God who feeds.

In our encounter with the metaphor of the God who feeds, we recognize something of the power of the metaphor to lure us into the world it imagines and to shape the way we view God and life in the world. Something of the power of the metaphor to stir the imagination was evident from the creative ways in which postbiblical interpreters used the metaphor of the God who feeds in their theological formulations. The imaginative depictions of the metaphor of the God who feeds in the biblical texts as well as in postbiblical interpretations provided a rich resource to imagine God creatively. In addition, as we will see in the following sections, the fact that the metaphor of the God who feeds bridges the testaments and subsequently finds expression in a vital Christian sacrament further adds to its appeal.

When Jesus Provides Food

An important trajectory of the metaphor of the God who feeds is that God's provision of food extends into the New Testament, where it became embodied in the figure of Jesus. This trajectory offers some important perspectives on the metaphor of the God who feeds and is, of course, responsible for the fact that the metaphor of the God who feeds did not merely remain an abstract theological expression but became concretized in the sacrament of the Eucharist. Although not an exhaustive treatment, this is an attempt to show how the metaphor of God providing food continued to be important throughout the Christian Scriptures. Some of the same themes and connotations of the metaphor we have seen thus far reappear in various New Testament texts; however, new circumstances called for fresh accents that caused the metaphor to develop in new directions. To illustrate this, I will make a few brief comments on how the Gospels of Luke and John use the metaphor of the God who provides food by means of Jesus.

Providing Food in the Gospel of Luke

In the Gospel of Luke, one could describe Jesus' entire ministry as providing food to the hungry. It is significant that Jesus' provision of food is a direct continuation of the metaphor of the God who feeds. For instance, the Magnificat (Luke 1:46-55) depicts *God* as filling the hungry with good things (Luke 1:53). Jesus' ministry becomes a concrete expression of this promise. The Beatitudes in Luke 6:21 tell of Jesus blessing the hungry (οἱ πεινῶντες), promising that they will be satisfied. Throughout Luke's Gospel there are signs that Jesus makes good on this promise, such as the miraculous feeding stories where Jesus feeds a huge crowd with five fishes and two loaves (Luke 9:10-17; see also the parallel stories in Matt 14:15-21, Mark 6:35-44, John 6:5-15).

It is important to note that God's provision of food underlies Jesus' act of feeding the crowd in Luke 9:10-17. Several scholars identify the correspondence between these stories that are told to describe Jesus' ministry and the texts dealing with God's provision of manna in the wilderness (Exod 16; Num 11).[1] Like God, Jesus provides food to the people in a desolate place (ἐν ἐρήμῳ τόπῳ in Luke 9:12), evoking memories of the provision of manna in the wilderness, where the Israelites had only God's provision to rely on for survival. And, like God's provision of food, there is more than enough for everyone, even leftovers, symbolizing the abundance of God's provision of food. The feeding story in Luke 9 further evokes the metaphor of the God who feeds in that, although it is Jesus who feeds the people, Jesus recognizes God as the gracious benefactor of the hungry people when he looks up to heaven to thank God for the food (Luke 9:16). As Joel Green notes, "Jesus himself is presented, then, as the one through whom God's benefaction is present."[2] In other words, God feeds the people by means of Jesus.

The link between Jesus' and God's provision of food is also seen in the contrast between Jesus' and the disciples' view of the source of the food. Whereas the disciples want to send the crowd away to buy food in the nearby towns (vv. 12-13), the food that Jesus provides is free, echoing the words of Isa 55:1-2. Earlier we saw how God graciously extended an invitation to come, buy, and eat the very best gifts of food without money—an invitation that is continued by Jesus' act of providing food.

However, Luke 9 develops the metaphor of the God who feeds in a new direction when the disciples are called to feed the hungry (Luke 9:13). When they complain that they do not have enough food to do this, Jesus feeds the multitudes, but it is the *disciples* who are given the task to hand out the food (Luke 9:16). This command of Jesus to the disciples to distribute the food implies that the disciples are called to bring to fruition something of God's provision of food in the world.

Providing Food in the Gospel of John

Also the Gospel of John places special emphasis on the food that Jesus offers. One sees this in the miracle of the wine (2:1-11), the living water that gives life (4:10-14), the feeding of the multitude (6:1-15), the bread from heaven (6:22-59) that is interpreted to be the bread of life, and finally the miracle of the abundance of fish that Jesus provides in John 21:1-14.[3] It is interesting to note that food marks the beginning and the end of Jesus' public career in the Gospel of John. So, in John 2:1-11, the miracle of the wine serves as a sign of the coming of the kingdom of God in the person of Jesus. And in John 21:1-14, it seems as if the breakfast by the shore, consisting of bread and fish, harks back to the previous time Jesus provided the people with a meal of fish and bread (John 6:1-15). This final meal may suggest that this crucified and exalted Jesus in your midst is the Bread of Life.

When considering Jesus' provision of food in the Gospel of John, it is important to keep in mind the many connections that scholars have identified between Jesus' provision of food in the Gospel of John and Woman Wisdom's provision of food (cf., e.g., Prov 9 and Sir 24). For instance, like Woman Wisdom, Jesus speaks in long discourse using the first-person pronoun and invites people to come, eat, and drink from the gifts of food that he offers. It seems as if the biblical metaphor of the God who feeds, as enriched by Woman Wisdom's provision of food (cf. ch. 5), provides key categories to speak about Jesus' ministry and life. This is particularly evident in John 6, where Jesus' provision of food is directly related to the metaphor of the God who feeds. We see this in Jesus' explanation of the food multiplication in verses 26-33. In a style of argumentation that reminds one of a Jewish midrash (cf. ch. 1), Jesus tries to correct the crowd's misunderstanding in verse 32: Do not read *Moses* gave you bread in the wilderness but, rather, read *God* gave you bread to eat.[4] Jesus critiques the crowd's misunderstanding that Moses is the one who miraculously provided manna in the wilderness. Thus, John implies that Jesus is the second Moses who will feed them as before. The crowd mistakenly regards Jesus as a miracle worker who fed them with mortal food but misses the greater significance of Jesus' gifts of food that give eternal life. As in the case of Woman Wisdom, Jesus' provision of food is meant to evoke the presence of the Giver.

However, after Jesus has identified the Giver, he now identifies himself as the given, when he describes himself as the Bread of Life (v. 35). To eat and drink from the food that Jesus offers is to become fully united with God. Thus, to share in his life-giving gifts becomes an expression of having communion with Jesus as the divine presence.[5]

Within this depiction, one hears Woman Wisdom's voice, inviting people to come share her gifts of food. Similar to Woman Wisdom's invitation to come eat and drink, the Johannine Jesus, who has been identified as Logos/Sophia incarnate, offers himself as the bread that truly gives life to believers. It is significant that in both John 6 and Sir 24, the one who provides food is also depicted as the food itself. But whereas Woman Wisdom's gifts of food lead to an unquenchable hunger and thirst, those who eat from Jesus' gifts of food will never be hungry and thirsty again.

This close connection between Woman Wisdom and Jesus provides scholars with the opportunity to develop the female dimension of the divine. Elizabeth Johnson argues in this regard, "In Jesus Christ we encounter the mystery of God who is neither male nor female, but who as source of both and Creator of both in the divine image can in turn be imaged as either."[6] Johnson sees in the figure of Jesus Christ Sophia "a healthy blend of female and male imagery that empowers everyone, and works beautifully to symbolize" this one God.[7]

Judith McKinlay strongly reacts concerning Johnson's notion of "a healthy blend of female and male imagery." She argues that once one reaches the Gospel of John, the female dimension of Wisdom has been completely subsumed into the male figure of Jesus, so that rather there is a shameless scarcity of female imagery. For instance, in the prologue of John, one finds that Jesus is explicitly connected to the male terminology of Logos (the Word), even though the language and imagery used to describe Jesus in the prologue as in the rest of the book is very much that of Woman Wisdom. For McKinlay, even if there are still traces of Woman Wisdom, "they now lie in the shadow of the male son of the divine." She rightly notes that the implications are no doubt substantial.[8]

McKinlay's critique is valid indeed. However, as in chapter 5, the question is whether one can reclaim these female traces in a conscious act of allowing the "age-old voice of the feminine to be heard once more" or whether one can look through the maleness of Jesus seeing how Woman Wisdom serves as a legitimate expression of the God who feeds her children.[9] This will of course require a deliberate act of interpretation on the part of the reader, who is guided by the numerous benefits of such an interpretation. For instance, to do so would indeed deepen our understanding of the mystery of God who created both male and female in

God's image and contribute to a greater sense of the equal worth of both male and female in the eyes of God.

WHEN A METAPHOR BECOMES A SACRAMENT

The New Testament appropriation of the metaphor of the God who feeds, and particularly the texts that narrate Jesus' role as host in the Last Supper (Luke 22:17-20 and the parallel passages in Matt 26:26-29 and Mark 14:22-25; see also 1 Cor 11:23-25), contributed to the development of the Eucharist, or what is called depending on one's tradition, the Lord's Supper, Communion, Mass, or Breaking of the Bread. At some moment in time, the metaphor became ritualized into the habitual actions of what David Ford calls the "eucharistic practice."[10] This action of thoughtfully interweaving the world that Scripture imagines with the liturgical practices of the church has made the metaphor of the God who feeds tremendously powerful.

Since the sacrament of the Eucharist is where most people encounter the metaphor of the God who feeds, it may be fitting to draw this book to a close by introducing some perspectives on the Eucharist. There is indeed a profusion of viewpoints on this sacrament; most fruitful are the debates carried on within the ecumenical endeavor to find common ground (cf., e.g., the ecumenical document, "Baptism, Eucharist, Ministry").[11] Although these concluding remarks should not be understood as speaking the last word on the many complex issues regarding this sacrament that have kept people occupied and at odds for centuries, we will see in the following comments how the ecumenical expression of the Eucharist shows a close affinity to the associations that have surfaced in this book concerning the metaphor of God's provision of food. In this regard, it is significant to observe how the powerful biblical depictions of God's provision of food receive a sacramental quality in the Eucharist.

"Baptism, Eucharist, Ministry" describes the meaning of the Eucharist in terms of the following aspects: First, the Eucharist is *"a proclamation and a celebration of the work of God"* (BEM 2A3). In this book, we have seen a composite picture of God who graciously feeds God's children—something which is central to the celebration and proclamation of God's work in the Eucharist. These gracious and loving actions of God invite response. One way of responding would be to thank and praise God for God's goodness. As "Baptism, Eucharist, Ministry" states, "the eucharist is the benediction (berekah) by which the Church expresses its thankfulness for all God's benefits" (2A3). Or in David Ford's words, in thanksgiving "the past is repeated in such a way that it is fruitful in a new way for the present and future."[12] This fruitful way of living is expressed most poignantly in the call to respond to God's love, as expressed by God's provision of food, by entering into joy.

Second, the theme of *remembrance* is central to the celebration of the Eucharist (BEM 2B5-7). In it, believers are encouraged to remember how the Lord Jesus, on the night he was betrayed, took bread and, after he had given thanks, broke it and said, "This is my body that is for you. Do this in remembrance of me" (1 Cor 11:23-25; cf. Matt 26:26-29; Mark 14:22-25; Luke 22:14-20).

Building on the work of Jan Assmann, Michael Welker shows how the biblical canon makes possible a shared identity—a "living cultural memory" that exhibits astounding power. In addition, the wealth of perspectives contained in the canonical traditions "stimulates a vitality of ongoing interpretations," which energize the participants to embrace the richness of the world behind the ritual.[13]

This perspective is also true of the metaphor of the God who feeds that we have discovered thus far. One could say that the occurrences of the God who feeds form part of the memory embedded in the Eucharist, or what Luke Johnson called "the world Scripture imagines."[14] The various expressions of the metaphor of God's provision of food serve as a rich resource in the call to remembrance. The God who has made possible the salvific work in Jesus Christ *is* the God who feeds. In the ritual of the Eucharist, believers are called to remember how God's provision of food is continued in the actions of Jesus feeding the multitudes and breaking the bread in the Last Supper. To remember the rich biblical depictions concerning the God who feeds when celebrating the Eucharist enriches our understanding of God as well as the significance of the sacrament we celebrate.

An important part of the call to remembrance echoes something of the memories of pain and suffering discussed earlier in this book. Welker points out that the center of the Eucharist refers us to Jesus' suffering and dying. We see this in the references to the "broken, torn, divided, utterly given bread," the "shed blood," as well as the associations of "death and mourning, guilt and shame" that are evoked by the cross. For Welker, this is evidence that God chooses to associate with the pain of this world.[15] Or as Ford describes this aspect of God's character, "God whose way of being God is to be involved in the contingencies in a shockingly complete and painful way."[16]

These reminders of the brokenness of the world around us should always be a vital part of the celebration of the Eucharist. As we are celebrating the God who feeds, we should not forget that for more than 800 million people in the world, this claim means nothing if the words are not accompanied by actions. To partake in the Eucharist means that we commit ourselves to making something of the claim that God feeds *all* of creation come true for those who still are suffering from hunger. Moreover, the Eucharist encourages us to notice those we willfully and unintentionally exclude from the table. We are called to find ways in which we can invite them to come share in God's goodness and, even more important, find ways in which they can feel at home.

Third, "Baptism, Eucharist, Ministry" notes that through the Holy Spirit *"the historical words of Jesus" are made "present and alive"* (BEM 2C14). This statement relates to the much-disputed "real presence" of Christ in the Eucharist, which undoubtedly means different things to different people, depending on one's denomination.[17] Regardless of what different believers may have in mind when talking about God's presence in Jesus Christ in the Eucharist, "Baptism, Eucharist, Ministry," agrees that God's presence by means of the Spirit is a central aspect of the Eucharist. The presence of God does make a difference in people's lives. In this book, we see time and again how people particularly saw in God's gifts of food something of God's real presence with them. All the more, in the Eucharist, the piece of bread and sip of wine serve as reminders of God's presence in God's gifts of food. The Eucharist thus serves as the space where we are called to recognize God's presence and to trust the Gracious Provider for our daily bread in every facet of our lives.

Fourth, "Baptism, Eucharist, Ministry" describes the Eucharist as *the communion of the faithful,* thus "it is in the eucharist that the community of God's people is fully manifested." The church is called to work toward "reconciliation and sharing among all those regarded as brothers and sisters in the one family of God" (BEM 2D19-20). This perspective closely relates to a key theme of this book. A central aspect of the metaphor of the God who feeds is that God's provision of food is all-inclusive, extending to all of creation. This is nowhere more evident than in the communal meal around the table where all believers are welcome. David Ford formulates this perspective: "The vision is of everyone around the same table, face to face. Even to imagine sitting together like that gently but inexorably exposes injustice, exploitation, sexism, hardheartedness, and the multiple ways of rejecting the appeal in the face of the other."[18]

The Eucharist becomes the place where people are encouraged to participate in making the metaphor of God's provision of food a reality by feeding the hungry, working toward finding solutions for famine in the world, and breaking down the barriers of racism, injustice, and separation, which all contribute to the gross inequality in the world today seen in the huge gap between rich and poor.[19] The Eucharist exhibits a strong appeal as it serves as a visual sign of the believer's commitment to participate in this call to make the world a better place.

Finally, "Baptism, Eucharist, Ministry" describes the Eucharist as the *"Meal of the Kingdom,"* in which the church "joyfully celebrates and anticipates the coming of the Kingdom in Christ" (BEM 2E22). But as Welker realistically points out, "in the celebration of the Supper, the church knows that it is still underway," that the "'heavenly eucharist' still lies in the distance."[20] We therefore anticipate the full realization of God's kingdom, looking forward with longing to a time when God's provision of food will become a reality for all people. We have seen strong evidence of this expectation in chapter 4, where the faithful held fast to the hope of a better tomorrow even as they were experiencing the pain of lack in their lives. In the celebration of the Eucharist, we look forward to the heavenly banquet where all will be gathered around the table with food aplenty to eat.

CONCLUSION: ASSESSING THE VALUE OF THE FEMALE METAPHOR OF THE GOD WHO FEEDS

We have seen in this book how there is suggestive evidence for imagining the metaphor of the God who feeds in female terms. This is particularly evident in chapter 1, where a metaphor of nursing was fruitfully used by interpreters to describe God's provision of food. In the rest of this book, we have engaged in a process of creatively reimagining the various dimensions of the metaphor of God who feeds in female terms. This metaphor may at first create an experience of shock on the part of the reader, as he or she may not be used to thinking about God in this way.

However, the appeal of this metaphor is situated in its genuine creativity so that within its ability to surprise lies the possibility of a new understanding of God. Particularly compelling metaphors may actually change the way we think, as well as the way we act. Without doubt, the most significant effect of understanding the metaphor of the God who feeds in terms of a female metaphor of motherhood is that it may challenge people to rethink their presuppositions that God is literally a male God who can be conceived only in terms of male imagery. Women's experience opens up exciting new possibilities of speaking about the mystery of God.

To use a metaphor of food and nursing to describe God's love is indeed a productive way of incorporating women's experience, which, until recently, has not featured significantly in the theological conversation. Throughout the centuries there have been strong associations between women and food, thus forming an integral part of women's experience. What's more, to imagine the metaphor of God as the Mother who feeds her children exhibits the potential to imagine God's love in a different way. There is something in the act of providing food to the young, and especially mothers nursing, that shows much promise for imagining God's care for us. We saw in chapter 1 how a number of texts presented the metaphor of a mother nursing her child as the best means to describe Israel's absolute dependence on God, as well as the all-sufficiency of God's care in manna. Similarly, the metaphor of a mother nursing her child may provide theological language to describe our own dependence on God, who provides for all of our needs. But it is not only the experience of nursing that can be useful in imagining God's love. We have seen throughout this book how other connotations of food may serve as a valuable resource to imagine God. For example, in addition to the notion of food as basic sustenance to keep our minds and bodies going, we have also seen the many pleasant associations of food that is often served at joyful occasions.

At this point, it is important to remind ourselves that we should not yield to the temptation of sentimentalizing maternal imagery of God, thereby creating stereotypes of what mothers are supposed to be. Maternal qualities are not limited to tenderness, softness, weakness, and passivity, and the act of "mothering" extends beyond the act of giving food. The maternal metaphor of God should be inclusive of a variety of characteristics not just nurturing ones. We saw evidence of this all throughout this book when the metaphor of God who feeds not only denotes a dimension of nurturing care but also contains a detailed depiction of God's anger and punishment of Israel, thereby creating the dimension of God disciplining her children. Similarly, the dimension of teaching also enhances our understanding of what maternal imagery could signify. Consequently, this multidimensional metaphor offers considerable benefits as it provides a rich perspective on mothering, potentially preventing the metaphor from falling into the snare of stereotyping. As Elizabeth Johnson argues: "There is more to being a woman than being a mother, even for women who are rearing children, even while that experience is crucially and irreplaceably important."[21] Mothering also influences other relationships in women's lives, including the roles of teacher and mentor, which further extends the definition of what it means to be a mother.

An important effect of imagining the metaphor of the God who feeds as a mother feeding her children may be that God is perceived in a different way. A maternal metaphor exhibits a lot of potential to change the way we speak about the mystery of God. The regular use of this metaphor may do much to portray God's love in terms of mutuality, beneficence, and empowerment, instead of the strict, authoritarian view that constitutes many people's picture for God.

On the other hand, one should not forget that a maternal metaphor of the divine could also exhibit authoritarian and patriarchal features.[22] One should, therefore, not fall into the snare of idealizing mothers. As many examples as there are of loving and reliable mothers, there are also instances of inadequate and abusive mothers. Mothers may be wrathful, moody, and obsessive; and, for some people, the image of mother may be just as problematic as father for others. A good example of this problem is found in chapter 3, where we saw how God withholds food—actions which very much could be perceived as abusive. To imagine the God who feeds in female terms may also have an effect on our human relationships. The compassionate, empowering love that is associated with a maternal metaphor for God is something that we should all work to develop—men and women, not just mothers. Such a perspective may do much to prevent an exclusionary attitude toward women who are not mothers, such as women unable to conceive or women who for various reasons decide not to have children. One needs to understand that "mothering" is not limited to the physical act of being a mother. Many of us have had female role models, such as teachers and friends, who "mothered" us in various ways. And increasingly, fathers rightly fulfill these nurturing roles with the effect that "fathering" also may gain the connotation of "lifelong, engaged, intimate caring."[23] Thus, the metaphor of God as Mother may make a claim on all who have experienced the joys of God's motherly love to continue to mother others.

These wonderful possibilities regarding the female metaphor of the God who feeds capture something of the power and allure embedded in this metaphor. However, the sad reality we have to face is that the church has suffered in countless ways from not regularly imaging God in female terms. Nowhere is this poverty of female imagery more evident than in the liturgy and, particularly, in the celebration of the Eucharist. For centuries, the celebrant of the Eucharist was a male priest or pastor, harking back to the male image of Jesus Christ as host. In some denominations today, this argument is still a vital part of the reason why females are not permitted to the ordained ministry.[24] However, as we have seen earlier, there is actually a strong connection between Jesus and Woman Wisdom, suggesting something of the female dimension of the divine we have seen in this book and raising questions as to how significant Jesus' gender is for the celebration of the Eucharist. One even finds some early church fathers who use the traditions of Woman Wisdom inviting people to a meal with food and wine that give life in reference to the celebration of the Eucharist. For instance, in a sermon on Prov 9:1, Hippolytus writes, "'And she hath furnished her table' ... also refers to His honoured and undefiled body and blood, which day by day are administered and offered sacrificially at the spiritual divine table, as a memorial of that first and ever-memorable table of the spiritual divine supper."[25]

However, these connections between Woman Wisdom and Jesus gradually receded into the background when Woman Wisdom disappeared into the male figure of Jesus. McKinlay rightly points out that, particularly concerning the Eucharist, "the change from female host to male" had considerable implications which still affects many people in both Christian and Jewish communities today.[26] There is something tragic about the many generations of men and women who have never seen a female pastor or priest serving the elements of bread and wine. What a difference it would make to have a female pastor or priest serve as host, acting as an embodied symbol of the God who gives food to all. In light of the emphasis of life, which runs like a golden thread throughout this book, how powerful would it be to have a pregnant celebrant whose own body vividly symbolizes the joy of the God who feeds, whose gifts of food and drink provide the ultimate gift—life!

The portrayal of the God who feeds in female terms invites the church to recover the female associations of the metaphor of the God as one who feeds her children like a mother. By embracing the rich biblical traditions from which this metaphor is derived and allowing oneself to be challenged by the imaginative portrayal of the God who feeds her children, we can enrich our relationship with God. Another way to recover these associations is to start using this metaphor in the liturgical and ecclesial practices of the church. Perhaps this metaphor of the God who feeds may transform the way we believers think about God and God's relationship to the world, our self-understanding, and our relationship with one another and all creation.

NOTES

Introduction

1. E. Hinkson, ed., *The Hymnal: Published by Authority of the General Assembly of the Presbyterian Church in the United States of America* (Philadelphia: The Presbyterian Board of Publication and Sabbath-School Work, 1896), no. 524.

2. Quoted in John E. Burkhart, "Reshaping Table Blessings: 'Blessing...and Thanksgiving...to Our God' (Rev 7:12)," *Interpretation* 48 (1994): 54. Cf. Louis Finkelstein, "The Birkat Ha-Mazon," *The Jewish Quarterly Review* 14 (1928–1929): 215-16.

3. Brian Wren, *What Language Shall I Borrow? God-Talk in Worship: A Male Response to Feminist Theology* (New York: Crossroad, 1989), 108-9.

4. It is a very difficult decision whether to use the term *Old Testament* or *Hebrew Bible*. There are good reasons for both, and scholars are sharply divided on this issue. On the one hand, one wants to show respect for Jewish interpreters with whom we share much, leading some scholars to strongly advocate the use of the term *Hebrew Bible*. After much deliberation, I hesitantly decided to use the term *Old Testament*. However, in light of the notion of dialogue that runs throughout this book, this is done with the deepest respect for other interpretative traditions.

5. Elizabeth A. Johnson, *She Who Is: The Mystery of God in Feminist Theological Discourse* (New York: Crossroad, 1992), 33-34.

6. Sallie McFague, "Mother God," in *The Power of Naming: A Concilium Reader in Feminist Liberation Theology* (ed. Elisabeth Schüssler Fiorenza; Maryknoll, N.Y.: Orbis Books, 1996), 324-29; *Models of God: Theology for an Ecological Nuclear Age* (Philadelphia: Fortress, 1987), 107-8.

7. Kim Chernin, *The Hungry Self: Women, Eating, and Identity* (New York: Times Books, 1985), 200.

8. At the outset, I should note that the meaning of the word *feminist* is not obvious. Feminists are accused of being blind to the fact that they represent a white, middle-class, first-world point of view. As a result, womanist and mujerista theology have claimed their unique perspectives, as have the contributions of Asian, Latin American, and African women. I argue that each woman has a limited voice. As it is difficult and even impossible to speak for others, the best one can do is to be open to dialogue. Thus, I will put forward my middle-class, white, African feminist voice, in the hope that other women and men will dialogue with me. Similarly, the concept of "women's experience" surely is not a unitary notion. Women of various cultures, races, and socioeconomic backgrounds have

very different experiences and perspectives to contribute. Nevertheless, there also may be a number of shared experiences that provide common ground, like the experience of being excluded because of one's gender.

9. Johnson, *She Who Is*, 39-40, 45, 47, 55; Johanna W. H. van Wijk-Bos, *Reimagining God: The Case for Scriptural Diversity* (Louisville: Westminster John Knox, 1995), 35.

10. Elisabeth Schüssler Fiorenza, *But She Said: Feminist Practices of Biblical Interpretation* (Boston: Beacon, 1992), 146.

11. See the bibliography for some selected examples.

12. Rita Nakashima Brock, "What Is a Feminist? Strategies for Change and Transformations of Consciousness," in *Setting the Table: Women in Theological Conversation* (ed. Rita Nakashima Brock et al.; St. Louis: Chalice, 1995), 12.

13. Schüssler Fiorenza, *But She Said*, 26, 73.

14. To mention two helpful treatments: Janet Martin Soskice, *Metaphor and Religious Language* (Oxford: Clarendon, 1985); Paul Avis, *God and the Creative Imagination: Metaphor, Symbol and Myth in Religion and Theology* (London: Routledge, 1999).

15. William P. Brown, *Seeing the Psalms: A Theology of Metaphor* (Louisville: Westminster John Knox, 2002); "The Metaphorical Imagination and Biblical Interpretation," in *God and the Imagination: A Primer to Reading the Psalms in an Age of Pluralism* (The 2000 J. J. Thiessen Lectures; Winnipeg, Manitoba: CMBC Publications, 2001); Leo Perdue, *Wisdom and Creation: The Theology of Wisdom Literature* (Nashville: Abingdon, 1994), 59-63.

16. Soskice, *Metaphor*, 49.

17. Avis, *God and the Creative Imagination*, 97. See P. N. Furbank, *Reflections on the Word "Image"* (London: Secker and Warburg, 1970), 1-12, 23.

18. Perdue, *Wisdom and Creation*, 62.

19. Marc Z. Brettler, "The Metaphorical Mapping of God in the Hebrew Bible," in *Metaphor, Canon and Community: Jewish, Christian and Islamic Approaches* (ed. Ralph Bisschops and James Francis; Bern: Peter Lang, 1999), 224. See also the work of William Brown who describes the interpretation of the metaphor as the "unpacking" of a metaphor, calling it "an open-ended, inexhaustible process that leads to ever increasing possibilities and connections" ("The Metaphorical Imagination," 14). Phyllis Trible does something similar in chapter 2 ("Journey of a Metaphor") of her book *God and the Rhetoric of Sexuality* when she suggests that a thread of female imagery for God runs through the Old Testament (OBT; Philadelphia: Fortress, 1978), 31-59.

20. For a more extensive presentation, see L. Juliana M. Claassens, "Biblical Theology as Dialogue: Continuing the Conversation on Bakhtin and Biblical Theology," *JBL* 122 (2003): 127-45.

21. Brettler makes an important observation concerning the use of history in his investigation of metaphorical language for God. He argues that although it may be true that YHWH shares many characteristics with the Canaanite deities Baal and El, an emphasis on history helps one to understand the history of Yahwism, but not Yahwism itself ("Metaphorical Mapping of God," 219).

22. Brevard S. Childs, *Introduction to the Old Testament as Scripture* (Philadelphia: Fortress, 1979), 76.

23. A good example of such an approach is Walter Brueggemann's *Theology of the Old Testament*, where he goes to great lengths in bringing what he calls the countertestimony of Israel into play. This provides him with a way of incorporating Wisdom, and particu-

larly the unconventional witness of Job and Ecclesiastes, into his Old Testament theology (*Theology of the Old Testament: Testimony, Dispute, Advocacy* [Minneapolis: Fortress, 1997], 386-99).

1. Manna from Heaven and Mother's Milk

1. In Num 11, there seem to be negative connotations to God's provision of food. In this regard, compare the proposal of reading the wilderness narratives in terms of a ring structure around Sinai. Whereas the manna and quail are gratefully accepted as God's gifts before Sinai, after Sinai the people complain about the monotony of the manna (v. 6) and the profusion of quail causes the people to become deathly ill (v. 33). Moreover, whereas God gives without hesitation in response to Israel's murmuring in Exod 16, in Num 11, God becomes exceedingly angry and punishes Israel for its complaint. Compare L. Juliana M. Claassens, "The God Who Feeds: A Feminist-Theological Analysis of Key Pentateuchal and Intertestamental Texts" (PhD diss., Princeton Theological Seminary, 2001), 103-4.

2. Marieke Den Hartog and M. Poorthuis, "Manna en Sabbat in de Rabbijnse Traditie" in *Brood uit de Hemel: Lijnen van Exodus 16 naar Johannes 6 tegen de Achtergrond van de Rabbijnse Literatuur* (ed. Wim Beuken et al.; Kampen: J. H. Kok, 1985), 118. See also Ps 131:2, which expresses this profound theological statement of total resignation and peace in God's presence. Patrick D. Miller has argued that, in light of the emphasis on women's experience, Ps 131 conceivably has been prayed by a woman (*They Cried to the Lord: The Form and Theology of Biblical Prayer* [Minneapolis: Fortress, 1994], 239-43).

3. It is very difficult to date the rabbinic traditions since many collections were only finalized in the fourth century and show signs of reworking by the final editor. Peter Schäfer remarks that the various rabbinic documents provide "no fixed frame of reference" in which the various documents can be placed in a chronological order, making it extremely difficult to ask historical questions of these texts ("Research into Rabbinic Literature: An Attempt to Define the Status Quaestionis," *JJS* 37 [1986]: 150).

4. Midrash can be defined as the careful study of a biblical passage, which it seeks to "search" (*daraš*) and explicate. Midrash is born out of an endeavor to actualize texts in light of contemporary circumstances, thus making the biblical texts relevant to a new generation of hearers. Moreover, a principal method the rabbis employed to clarify a biblical text was to insert parallel texts. The rabbis are thus constantly explaining Scripture by means of Scripture. For a comprehensive definition cf. Renée Bloch, "Midrash," in *Approaches to Ancient Judaism: Theory and Practice* (ed. William Scott Green; trans. Mary Howard Callaway; BJS; 5 vols.; Missoula, Mont.: Scholars Press for Brown University, 1978), 1:32.

5. James Kugel, "Two Introductions to Midrash," *Proof* 3 (1983): 145.

6. *Mek. Amalek* 3:180 (Lauterbach).

7. This is an interpretation by the translator (Jung) that has the purpose of clarifying the wordplay. This interpretation arises from the fact that the meaning of the word לשד is completely unknown, an uncertainty that is evident from both the ancient variants and modern translations. For example, the NRSV has "cakes baked with oil" (cf. LXX), the NIV has "something made with olive oil" (an honest admission of ignorance), and the NJPS has "rich cream." For a description of the various textual variants see Claassens, "The God Who Feeds," 67-68.

8. Leo Jung, trans., *Yoma, Sukkah, Bezah* (vol. 3 of *Seder Mo'ed* of the Babylonian Talmud; ed. I. Epstein; London: Soncino Press, 1978), *b. Yoma 75a*. The bracketed material in the quotation appears in the original work.

9. *Sifre Num.* 89 (Neusner).

10. *Exod. Rab.* 1:12 (Lehrman).

11. William H. C. Propp, "Milk and Honey: Biblical Comfort Food," *BR* 15 (1999): 16, 54.

12. Compare, e.g., Sir 39:26, which regards honey, together with water, fire, iron, salt, wheat flour, milk, the blood of the grape, oil, and clothing as part of the basic necessities of human life.

13. Ivan G. Marcus, *Rituals of Childhood: Jewish Acculturation in Medieval Europe* (New Haven: Yale University Press, 1996), 88. The idea that olive trees and bees occur in the wild does not exclude later human activities like olive cultivation and oil processing. Compare, e.g., Frank S. Frick, "'Oil from Flinty Rock' (Deuteronomy 32:13): Olive Cultivation and Olive Oil Processing in the Hebrew Bible—A Socio-materialist Perspective," in *Food and Drink in the Biblical Worlds* (*Semeia* 86; ed. Athalya Brenner and Jan Willem van Henten; Atlanta: SBL, 1999), 1-18.

14. Johanna W. H. van Wijk-Bos, *Reimagining God: The Case for Scriptural Diversity* (Louisville: Westminster John Knox, 1995), 70.

15. A few words should be said about the terms that are used in Num 11:12. The female imagery and its implications are not evident to everyone. Many scholars have overlooked the nursing imagery, calling Moses a "nursing father." Compare, e.g., Benjamin D. Sommer, "Reflecting on Moses: The Redaction of Numbers 11," *JBL* 118 (1999): 611; Baruch Levine, *Numbers: A New Translation with Introduction and Commentary* (AB 4; New York: Doubleday, 1993), 312-13. Although the term אמן could be used for both men and women who care for dependent children, the term "suckling" or "nursing child" (ינק) bestows a female meaning on this term, as a nursing child needs nourishment in order to survive. Alfred Jepsen, אמן; *'āman*" *TDOT* 1:294; Ringgren, "ינק," *TDOT* 6:107; Dromeris, "ינק," *NIDOTTE* 2:472.

16. Mayer I. Gruber, "Breast-feeding Practices in Biblical Israel and in Old Babylonian Mesopotamia," in *Semitic Studies in Memory of Moshe Held* (ed. Edward L. Greenstein and David Marcus; New York: Jewish Theological Seminary, 1989), 70-71, 74-75.

17. This argument has been worked out elsewhere in much greater detail, where I show how the narrative details of the texts in which the metaphor occurs work together to create a multilayered picture of the metaphor of God providing food to her children. See Claassens, "The God Who Feeds," 102-201.

18. This portrayal of God relates to the particular setting of Numbers. Dennis T. Olson notes that the setting of Numbers has moved after the Sinai event to the wilderness of Sinai. God is no longer speaking from the top of the mountain but from the portable tent of meeting (*The Death of the Old and the Birth of the New: The Framework of the Book of Numbers and the Pentateuch* [Chico, Calif.: Scholars Press, 1985], 48).

19. For a further depiction of God using food, which ordinarily is considered to be a blessing, as punishment, cf. the image in Jer 8:14 and 9:15 where God is depicted as providing "poisoned water" to the people and giving them "wormwood" to eat. Robert P. Carroll describes, in strong terms, God as the "berserker god" who kills his own people "by means of deceptive hospitality" ("YHWH's Sour Grapes: Images of Food and Drink in the Prophetic Discourses of the Hebrew Bible," in *Food and Drink in the Biblical Worlds* [*Semeia* 86; ed. Athalya Brenner and Jan Willem van Henten; Atlanta: SBL, 1999], 123).

20. Dennis T. Olson, *Deuteronomy and the Death of Moses: A Theological Reading* (Minneapolis: Fortress, 1994), 141-42. The metaphor of God as warrior is quite common in the ancient Near East. Whereas God is normally said to fight for the people, in the Song of Moses it becomes clear that God is also free to fight against them when they forget the Rock that gave birth to them.

21. A series of reversals, identified by Dennis Olson in the Song of Moses, contributes to this interpretation of God's blessing turning into a curse. These reversals move from a pastoral introduction of soothing images to an "antipastoral" portrayal of chaotic and destructive forces (*Deuteronomy and the Death of Moses*, 146).

22. Patrick D. Miller, *Deuteronomy* (IBC; Louisville: John Knox, 1990), 233-34. Miller notes that this imagery should not be ignored or exaggerated. It is one of the ways the Old Testament talks about God in the vernacular of its time. God's vengeance has two sides to it. Sometimes it is rightful punishment, but sometimes it is used to describe the lifting up of the weak.

23. Carol Meyers, *Discovering Eve: Ancient Israelite Women in Context* (New York: Oxford University Press, 1988), 145-47. Meyers bases this statement on a comparative study of preindustrial societies. Such an approach is not without difficulties, as has been well noted. But because of the limited resources available on women's history, these difficulties may be inevitable. See also Phyllis Bird, "Women's Religion in Ancient Israel," in *Women's Earliest Records from Ancient Egypt and Western Asia* (ed. Barbara Lesko; Atlanta: Scholars Press, 1989), 287, 293.

24. In this regard, one may note that there never was a "golden age of matriarchy" in Israel. Nor were there liberating moments that have been pushed aside by patriarchalization. One finds, rather, a fluctuation side by side between liberation and suppression, power and powerlessness. The reality is that in many preindustrial societies, women can do a great deal of the economic work and support the basic economic roles in a society and yet still not be valued as equal. Israelite society was no different in this regard. Compare the response of Carol Delaney to Carol Meyers, "Women and the Domestic Economy of Early Israel," in *Women's Earliest Records from Ancient Egypt and Western Asia* (ed. Barbara Lesko; Atlanta: Scholars Press, 1989), 279.

25. Compare Leo G. Perdue, "The Household, Old Testament Theology, and Contemporary Hermeneutics," in *Families in Ancient Israel* (The Family, Religion, Culture; ed. Leo G. Perdue et al.; Louisville: Westminster John Knox, 1997), 225.

26. Walter Brueggemann, "A Subversive Memory in a Sacramental Container," *RefLitM* 19 (1985): 34-35.

27. Brueggemann, "A Subversive Memory," 35; Sallie McFague, *Models of God: Theology for an Ecological Nuclear Age* (Philadelphia: Fortress, 1987), 122.

28. In rabbinic literature a distinction is made between exegetical and homiletical midrashim. An exegetical midrash follows the structure of the biblical book and thus functions as a kind of running commentary. A homiletical midrash gives a close interpretation of selected passages of Scripture, which customarily followed the cycle of Scripture readings in the regular Sabbath service or festival days. Addison G. Wright, *The Literary Genre Midrash* (New York: Alba House, 1967), 52, 57.

29. *Cant. Rab.* 4:5 (Simon).

30. For the connections between Torah, Wisdom, and food imagery in rabbinic interpretation, cf., e.g., *Gen. Rab.* 70:5, 43:6, 54:1; *Num. Rab.* 8:9, 13:15, 16; *Eccl. Rab.* 7:8.

31. For more detail on a possible wisdom setting for Deut 32, see Claassens, "The God

Who Feeds," 124-27; Miller, *Deuteronomy*, 225-28. See also Olson's description of the form of Deuteronomy as a program of "catechesis," implying a process of education in faith from one generation to another (*Deuteronomy and the Death of Moses*, 2, 10-11).

32. The notion of God as the giver of life is powerfully summarized in the conclusion of the Song, when God emphatically states in v. 39: "I kill and I give life" (אני אמית ואחיה).

33. Joseph A. Fitzmyer bases his translation on Origen's explanation, "our bread for subsistence" (*The Gospel according to Luke X-XXIV* [AB 28A; New York: Doubleday, 1985], 896, 900). Joel Green rightly points out that the phrase "daily bread" (τὸν ἄρτον .... τὸ καθ' ἡμέραν) is much debated, but he also chooses it for his translation: "the bread needed for the rest of today." Joel B. Green, *The Gospel of Luke* (NICNT; Grand Rapids, Mich.: Eerdmans, 1997), 442; Luke T. Johnson, *The Gospel of Luke* (Collegeville, Minn.: Liturgical Press, 1991), 178.

34. Göran Larsson, *Bound for Freedom: The Book of Exodus in Jewish and Christian Traditions* (Peabody, Mass.: Hendrickson, 1999), 117.

35. Rolf P. Knierim, *The Task of Old Testament Theology: Substance, Method, and Cases* (Grand Rapids, Mich.: Eerdmans, 1995), 227.

36. Larsson, *Bound for Freedom*, 118. See also Brueggemann, "A Subversive Memory," 37.

37. Knierim, *The Task of Old Testament Theology*, 227.

38. Character ethics have become increasingly important in recent years. One of the questions pondered by theologians and biblical theologians is how the character of God may influence moral behavior. Compare, e.g., Bruce C. Birch, "Moral Agency, Community, and the Character of God in the Hebrew Bible," *Semeia* 66 (1994): 29; William P. Brown, *Character in Crisis: A Fresh Approach to the Wisdom Literature of the Old Testament* (Grand Rapids, Mich.: Eerdmans, 1996), 7-8.

39. *Paed* I.6.46.1 (ANF 2:221), as quoted in and modified by Kathleen E. McVey, "In Praise of Sophia: The Witness of Tradition," in *Women, Gender, and Christian Community* (ed. Jane Dempsey Douglass and James F. Kay; Louisville: Westminster John Knox, 1997), 40.

40. Although there is some uncertainty concerning the dating and setting of the *Odes*, most scholars now agree that these poems originated somewhere in Syria from around the mid-second century. The consensus further accepts the *Odes* as Christian, although the jury is still out on whether or not they are of a Gnostic nature. Susan Ashbrook Harvey rightly points out that the *Odes* stem from a multicultured Mediterranean world in which there was considerable interplay between religions resulting in a fluidity in the imagery and themes that are used ("The Odes of Solomon," in *Searching the Scriptures: A Feminist Commentary* [ed. Elisabeth Schüssler Fiorenza; 2 vols.; New York: Crossroad, 1994], 2:88, 93).

41. *Odes Sol.* 19:1-5 (Charlesworth).

42. Compare Carolyn Walker Bynum, *Holy Feast and Holy Fast: The Religious Significance of Food to Medieval Women* (Berkeley: University of California Press, 1987). Bynum has done an extensive study on food symbolism in the Middle Ages and provides a comprehensive overview of the images used in this time. See also her other work in *Jesus as Mother: Studies in the Spirituality of the High Middle Ages* (Berkeley: University of California Press, 1982).

43. Marcus, *Rituals of Childhood*, 88. See also 7, 55-56. The employment of these metaphors is not without problems and should therefore be treated with caution. Marcus's

study carefully shows that these rituals were found in different manifestations depending on the various contexts of medieval Europe, reminding us to be careful of generalizations. Another question raises the possibility that these Jewish traditions developed in reaction to the Christian eucharistic symbols, thus maintaining that the Torah, and not Jesus, is the true bread, the true manna, the true gift of milk and honey. These historical questions have no simple answers. Nevertheless, these rituals show some suggestive evidence that food or nursing language has been used to describe a life dedicated to learning.

44. Janet Martin Soskice, *Metaphor and Religious Language* (Oxford: Clarendon, 1985), 73, 88-90.

2. Feeding All of Creation

1. Karl Löning and Erich Zenger, *To Begin with, God Created: Biblical Theologies of Creation* (trans. Omar Kaste; Collegeville, Minn.: Liturgical Press, 2000), 21; Bernhard W. Anderson, *From Creation to New Creation: Old Testament Perspectives* (OBT; Minneapolis: Fortress, 1994), 31.

2. Walter Brueggemann, *Theology of the Old Testament: Testimony, Dispute, Advocacy* (Minneapolis: Fortress, 1997), 339.

3. Löning and Zenger, *To Begin with, God Created*, 40. See also Eccl 9:7 where the call to enjoy life is expressed in terms of similar food items.

4. Patrick D. Miller Jr., "The Poetry of Creation: Psalm 104," in *God Who Creates: Essays in Honor of W. Sibley Towner* (ed. William P. Brown and S. Dean McBride Jr.; Grand Rapids, Mich.: Eerdmans, 2000), 97-98.

5. James L. Mays, "'Maker of Heaven and Earth': Creation in the Psalms," in *God Who Creates: Essays in Honor of W. Sibley Towner* (ed. William P. Brown and S. Dean McBride Jr.; Grand Rapids, Mich.: Eerdmans, 2000), 84; Miller, "The Poetry of Creation," 99.

6. Carol A. Newsom, "The Moral Sense of Nature: Ethics in the Light of God's Speech to Job," *PSB* 15 (1994): 22.

7. Othmar Keel, *Jahwes Entgegnung an Hiob* (Göttingen: Vandenhoeck und Ruprecht, 1978).

8. Newsom, "The Moral Sense of Nature," 25.

9. Hans-Joachim Kraus, *Psalms 60-150: A Commentary* (trans. Hilton C. Oswald; Minneapolis: Augsburg, 1989), 557.

10. Siegfried Risse, "'Wir Sind die Jungen Raben!' Zur Auslegunsgeschichte von Ps. 147:9b," *BibInt* 7 (1999): 369, 374.

11. Joel B. Green, *The Gospel of Luke* (NICNT; Grand Rapids, Mich.: Eerdmans, 1997), 492; John Nolland, *Luke 9:21-18:34* (WBC; Dallas: Word Books, 1989), 692.

12. See also Job 38:39-41 where God's provision of food is clearly linked to the lion's and raven's action of hunting for prey.

13. David Alexander, "Feeding the Hungry and Protecting the Environment," in *All Creation Is Groaning: An Interdisciplinary Vision for Life in a Sacred Universe* (ed. Carol J. Demsey and Russell A. Butkus; Collegeville, Minn.: Liturgical Press, 2001), 78; *Sixth World Food Survey* (Rome: Food and Agriculture Organization of the United Nations, 1996). Alexander notes that most of these starving people live in the developing countries of Africa, Asia, and Latin America, where one person in five suffers from food inadequacy, i.e., ingesting fewer calories than the average adult requires for normal daily activities.

14. Michelle Mary Lelwica, *Starving for Salvation: The Spiritual Dimensions of Eating Problems among American Girls and Women* (New York: Oxford University Press, 1999), 20. Lelwica notes that up to 20 percent of college women suffer from anorexia and/or bulimia. The percentage of women who experienced trouble eating is even higher. See also Leanne Sue Simmons, "Taking Back the Body: Eating Disorders, Feminist Theological Ethics and Christic Gynodicy" (PhD diss., Princeton Theological Seminary, 2001).

15. There is an interesting link between the hunger for knowledge and hunger for food. See Judith E. McKinlay, "To Eat or Not to Eat: Where Is Wisdom in This Choice," in *Food and Drink in the Biblical Worlds* (*Semeia* 86; ed. Athalya Brenner and Jan Willem van Henten; Atlanta: SBL, 1999), 75.

16. Phyllis Trible, *God and the Rhetoric of Sexuality* (OBT; Philadelphia: Fortress, 1978), 87. McKinlay has done some intriguing work concerning the image of God as Trickster, "who both proscribes the fruit but who all along intends humankind to have the knowledge that it gives" ("To Eat or Not to Eat," 74-77).

17. Carol Meyers describes the interpretation history of this text, in which an anti-female bias seems to reign supreme (*Discovering Eve: Ancient Israelite Women in Context* [New York: Oxford University Press, 1988], 74-78). See also the work of Phyllis Trible, who challenges some of these "misreadings." She says that in Gen 2–3, man and woman are "equal in responsibility and in judgment, in shame and in guilt, in redemption and in grace. What the narrative says about the nature of woman it also says about the nature of man" ("Eve and Adam: Genesis 2–3 Reread," in *Womanspirit Rising: A Feminist Reader in Religion* [ed. Carol P. Christ and Judith Plaskow; San Francisco: HarperSanFrancisco, 1992], 78-79).

18. One should be careful not to collapse the distinction between illness and sin. There are of course numerous factors that contribute to eating disorders other than the society's fascination with the perfect body.

19. Norman C. Habel, *The Book of Job* (Philadelphia: Westminster, 1985), 538. See also Ps 104:26 where the Leviathan becomes the aquatic pet with which God plays, or as Miller calls it, "God's rubber duck in the great ocean bathtub" ("The Poetry of Creation," 98).

20. Habel, *Job*, 65. See also Miller, "The Poetry of Creation," 98.

21. Habel, *Job*, 534. See also Wendy Farley, *Tragic Vision and Divine Compassion: A Contemporary Theodicy* (Louisville: Westminster/John Knox, 1990), 60-61.

22. Bruce V. Malchow, "Contrasting Views of Nature," *Dialogue* 25 (1986): 40-43; Terence E. Fretheim, "Nature's Praise of God in the Psalms," *ExAud* 3 (1987): 28. See also the frank reference to "wickedness" in Ps 104:35. Mays notes that this verse should not be overlooked, as it honestly expresses the notion that wickedness is a shocking and unacceptable incongruence in God's world ("Maker of Heaven and Earth," 85).

23. *Midr. Tehillim* Ps 104.17 (Braude).

24. Norbert Lohfink, *Lobgesänge der Armen: Studien zum Magnifikat den Hodajot von Qumran und einige Späten Psalmen* (SBS 143; Stuttgart: Katholisches Bibelwerk, 1990), 118. See also Risse, "Wir Sind die Jungen Raben!" 385.

25. Walter Brueggemann, *Israel's Praise: Doxology against Idolatry and Ideology* (Philadelphia: Fortress, 1988), 94. See also Miller who proposes that to sing praises is a "powerful political act" (*They Cried to the Lord: The Form and Theology of Biblical Prayer* [Minneapolis: Fortress, 1994], 224).

26. Brueggemann, *Israel's Praise*, 98.

27. Frank Fromherz, "A Sense of Place," in *All Creation Is Groaning: An Interdisciplinary Vision for Life in a Sacred Universe* (ed. Carol J. Demsey and Russell A. Butkus; Collegeville, Minn.: Liturgical Press, 2001), 241.

28. *Midr. Tehillim* Ps 146.4 (Braude).

29. Katharine Doob Sakenfeld, *Ruth* (IBC; Louisville: John Knox, 1999), 45.

30. Ibid., 39.

31. Ibid., 46; Ellen van Wolde, *Ruth and Naomi* (trans. John Bowden; London: SCM Press, 1997), 40. Boaz commands his laborers to leave behind extra ears for Ruth—a gesture that van Wolde calls exceedingly generous, "an unprecedented initiative on the part of Boaz which causes surprise on both the part of the servants as well as the readers."

32. Sakenfeld, *Ruth*, 22.

33. *Midr. Tehillim* Ps 146.6 (Braude).

34. Newsom, "Moral Sense of Nature," 10.

35. See also Job 38:7, where the praise of creatures is linked directly with creation, and Pss 145–48, where God's works are called to praise. Claus Westermann, *Genesis 1-11: A Commentary* (trans. John J. Scullion; Minneapolis: Augsburg, 1984), 113, 166.

36. Risse, "Wir Sind die Jungen Raben!" 371, 380; Reinhard Gregor Kratz, "Die Gnade des täglichen Brots: Späte Psalmen auf dem Weg zum Vaterunser," *ZTK* 89 (1992): 15. See also Green, *Luke*, 492; Nolland, *Luke*, 692.

37. Green, *Luke*, 487, 494. The context of Luke 12:22-34 deals mainly with themes of finding one's security or allegiance in God, therefore addressing issues of poverty and wealth in an attempt to persuade the disciples and all those who care to listen to find their security in the caring God rather than in possessions.

38. Newsom, "The Moral Sense of Nature," 25, 27.

39. Anderson, *From Creation to New Creation*, 15; Löning and Zenger, *To Begin with, God Created*, 108.

40. Lynn White Jr., "The Historical Roots of Our Ecologic Crisis," *Science* 155 (1967): 1203-7; Anderson, *From Creation to New Creation*, 112. Walter Brueggemann points out in his *Theology of the Old Testament* (p. 454) that the work by Cameron Wybrow gives a helpful response to White's claims that the Bible provides the basis for exploiting the earth (*The Bible, Baconianism, and Mastery over Nature: The Old Testament and Its Modern Misreading* (American University Studies 7, Theology and Religion; vol. 112; New York: Peter Lang, 1991).

41. Farley, *Tragic Vision*, 69.

42. Elizabeth A. Johnson, *She Who Is: The Mystery of God in Feminist Theological Discourse* (New York: Crossroad, 1992), 171. See also Sallie McFague, *Models of God: Theology for an Ecological Nuclear Age* (Philadelphia: Fortress, 1987), 106-8.

43. Sallie McFague, *Life Abundant: Rethinking Theology and Economy for a Planet in Peril* (Minneapolis: Fortress, 2001), 146. See also McFague, *Models of God*, 86, 108.

3. When God Does Not Feed

1. Bruce C. Birch, *Hosea, Joel, and Amos* (Westminster Bible Companion; Louisville: Westminster John Knox, 1997), 134.

2. Graham S. Ogden and Richard R. Deutsch, *A Promise of Hope—A Call to Obedience: A Commentary on the Books of Joel and Malachi* (ITC; Grand Rapids, Mich.: Eerdmans, 1987), 20, 25-26.

3. Walter Harrelson, "Famine in the Perspective of Biblical Judgments and Promises," in *Lifeboat Ethics: The Moral Dilemmas of World Hunger* (ed. George R. Lucas and Thomas W. Ogletree; New York: Harper & Row, 1976), 84-87. See the work by Amartya Sen in *Poverty and Famines: An Essay on Entitlement and Deprivation*, where he argues that all famines are human made (Oxford: Oxford University Press, 1984).

4. Birch, *Hosea, Joel, and Amos*, 132.

5. Ogden and Deutsch, *A Promise of Hope*, 11.

6. Fabry notes that שׁוב seems to be a verb indicating movement and potentially signifies movement in the direction of the point of origin. However, this meaning is not set in stone, as the occurrence of שׁוב in Prov 20:26 seems to indicate. In this verse, שׁוב suggests movement without any specific direction. Accordingly, the theological usage of שׁוב, "return to God," is equally not automatic and, in its "pretheological phase," could well be understood as a liturgical act toward God (*TDOT* 7:1122).

7. Ogden and Deutsch, *A Promise of Hope*, 23.

8. Wendy Farley, *Tragic Vision and Divine Compassion: A Contemporary Theodicy* (Louisville: Westminster/John Knox, 1990), 20.

9. Ogden and Deutsch, *A Promise of Hope*, 21.

10. Kathleen O'Connor, "The Book of Lamentations: Introduction, Commentary, Reflection" in *The New Interpreter's Bible* (ed. Leander E. Keck et al.; 12 vols.; Nashville: Abingdon, 2001), 6:1020.

11. F. W. Dobbs-Allsopp, *Lamentations* (IBC; Louisville: John Knox, 2002), 51.

12. O'Connor, "Lamentations," 1021; Dobbs-Allsopp, *Lamentations*, 90.

13. Tod Linafelt, *Surviving Lamentations: Catastrophe, Lament and Protest in the Afterlife of a Biblical Book* (Chicago: University of Chicago Press, 2000), 56; Dobbs-Allsopp, *Lamentations*, 32.

14. Dobbs-Allsopp, *Lamentations*, 131.

15. O'Connor, "Lamentations," 1062; Linafelt, *Surviving Lamentations*, 308; Dobbs-Allsopp, *Lamentations*, 100.

16. O'Connor, "Lamentations," 1042-44; Dobbs-Allsopp, *Lamentations*, 42.

17. Birch, *Hosea, Joel, and Amos*, 143.

18. Ibid., 136, 140; Hans Walter Wolff, *Joel and Amos* (Hermeneia; trans. Waldemar Janzen et al.; ed. S. Dean McBride Jr.; Philadelphia: Fortress, 1977), 7.

19. Wolff, *Joel and Amos*, 327; James L. Mays, *Amos: A Commentary* (OTL; Philadelphia: Westminster, 1969), 145.

20. Harrelson, "Famine," 84, 91.

21. One should be careful that this spiritualization of famine does not lead us to avoid the larger issue of world famine. Although people's experience of personal suffering is undeniably important, people should be encouraged to also consider the pain of others. In this regard, Kathleen D. Billman and Daniel L. Migliore argue that Rachel, in Jer 31:15-17, becomes a model not only of crying about her own pain for losing her children but also about the injustice done to her children (*Rachel's Cry: Prayer of Lament and Rebirth of Hope* [Cleveland: United Church Press, 1999], 2).

22. Samuel E. Balentine, "Enthroned on the Praises and Laments of Israel," in *The Lord's Prayer: Perspectives for Reclaiming Christian Prayer* (ed. Daniel L. Migliore; Grand Rapids, Mich.: Eerdmans, 1993), 34.

23. Linafelt, *Surviving Lamentations*, 18-21. See also Dobbs-Allsopp, *Lamentations*, 2.

24. Dobbs-Allsopp, *Lamentations*, 3.

25. Ibid., 104.

26. Zachary Braiterman, *(God) after Auschwitz: Tradition and Change in Post-Holocaust Jewish Thought* (Princeton, N.J.: Princeton University Press, 1998), 31. This is in contrast with theodicy, which can be defined as an attempt to explain the presence of suffering in the world and God's role in it (p. 21).

27. Dobbs-Allsopp, *Lamentations*, 29-30.

28. Zvi Kolitz, *Yosl Rakover Talks to God* (trans. Carol Brown Janeway; New York: Pantheon Books, 1999). This story plays an interesting role in postholocaust reflection. Zachary Braiterman argues that Eliezer Berkovitz quotes the story of Yosl Rakover as an example of "authentic Jewish faith" in his book *With God in Hell*. Yosl Rakover is said to have been a Hasidic Jew whose wartime testimony was discovered in a small bottle in the ruins of the Warsaw ghetto. It is ironic that Berkovitz (like many other writers in the 1970s) quotes Rakover without apparently recognizing that Rakover is a fictitious character. Rakover's testimony was actually told by an Israeli writer named Zvi Kolitz, whose short story was first published after the war in a Yiddish newspaper in Buenos Aires, where after the story made its way to Israel, the United States, and Paris where it was presumed to be an authentic testimony. Braiterman, *(God) after Auschwitz*, 123-33.

29. Kolitz, *Yosl Rakover Talks to God*, 18-19.

30. Billman and Migliore, *Rachel's Cry*, 114.

31. David R. Blumenthal, *Facing the Abusing God: A Theology of Protest* (Louisville: Westminster/John Knox, 1993), xvi, 240-41. See also the depiction of God as a wife beater and an abusive parent in the rabbinic literature. For example, in *Exod. Rab.* 31:10 (Lehrman), the following example is used to describe God's relationship to Israel: "It can be compared to a man who was beating his wife. Her best friend asked him, 'How long will you go on beating her? If your desire is to drive her out, then keep on beating her till she dies; but if you do not wish her [to die], then why do you keep on beating her?'" (See also *Pesiq. Rab.* 8 [Braude and Kapstein]). And in *Pesiq. Rab Kah.* 15:4, God is depicted as a child killer, which presents, as Braiterman formulates, "a disturbing picture of God gone berserk"—*(God) after Auschwitz*, 53.

32. Blumenthal, *Facing the Abusing God*, 247-48; Dobbs-Allsopp, *Lamentations*, 44-45.

33. Walter Brueggemann, *The Hopeful Imagination: Prophetic Voices in Exile* (Philadelphia: Fortress, 1986), 41; Dobbs-Allsopp, *Lamentations*, 35.

34. Dobbs-Allsopp, *Lamentations*, 37. See also Billman and Migliore's important book *Rachel's Cry*, in which they make a plea for recovering lament in the worship of the church.

35. Kolitz, *Yosl Rakover Talks to God*, 20.

36. Sallie McFague, *Life Abundant: Rethinking Theology and Economy for a Planet in Peril* (Minneapolis: Fortress, 2001), 151.

37. Harrelson, "Famine," 84, 92.

38. Alan B. Durning, "Ending Poverty," in *A Worldwatch Institute Report on Progress Toward a Sustainable Society* (ed. Lester R. Brown; New York: W. W. Norton, 1990), 135; David Alexander, "Feeding the Hungry and Protecting the Environment," in *All Creation Is Groaning: An Interdisciplinary Vision for Life in a Sacred Universe* (ed. Carol J. Demsey and Russell A. Butkus; Collegeville, Minn.: Liturgical Press, 2001), 80.

39. Farley, *Tragic Vision*, 69, 88.

40. O'Connor, "Lamentations," 1044; Linafelt, *Surviving Lamentations*, 53; Farley, *Tragic Vision*, 39, 69.

41. Alexander, "Feeding the Hungry," 80, 91.

42. *Lam. Rab.* 24 (Cohen); Braiterman, *(God) after Auschwitz,* 50-51; Linafelt, *Surviving Lamentations,* 116.

43. Linafelt, *Surviving Lamentations,* 3, 58, 75.

44. O'Connor, "Lamentations," 1045. Compare the work of Carol Newsom, in which she sees Second Isaiah offering "a selective rereading of Lamentations in the service of the exilic community" ("Response to Norman K. Gottwald: Social Class and Ideology in Isa 40-55," *Semeia* 58 [1992]: 75).

45. M. Wenig and N. Janowitz, "Siddur Nashim" (unpublished), 37. Quoted in Blumenthal, *Facing the Abusing God,* 41.

46. Farley, *Tragic Vision,* 119.

47. Compare the analysis of the phenomenon of scapegoating in chapter 4 of the dissertation by David E. Janzen, "'Thus I Purified Them From All Things Foreign': The Scapegoating of Foreign Women in Ezra-Nehemiah" (PhD diss., Princeton Theological Seminary, 1999).

48. Kim Chernin, *The Hungry Self: Women, Eating, and Identity* (New York: Times Books, 1985), 103.

49. Leanne Sue Simmons rightly notes that one should not be too hard on mothers. They are part of a complex patriarchal system, trying to survive the "rigid limitations" set on their selfhood. As she formulates it: "Most mothers would give anything they could to help their daughters thrive. Indeed, in many cases what they have given was not too little, but too much" ("Taking Back the Body: Eating Disorders, Feminist Theological Ethics and Christic Gynodicy" (PhD diss., Princeton Theological Seminary, 2001), 41-42, 44, 91.

50. The image of God as an abusive mother shares a lot with biblical texts that portray God as an abusive husband. Ezekiel 16 tells the story of Jerusalem, an abandoned infant rescued by God. After she grew to sexual maturity, God married her, lavishing her with beautiful clothes and fine food (Ezek 16:13, 19). But Jerusalem betrays her husband, which leads to physical abuse, which, in Ezek 16:27, is directly associated with food when God reduces the rations of Jerusalem. Katheryn Pfisterer Darr notes that the use of female imagery is problematic, as it "depicts female sexuality as the object of male possession and control, presents physical abuse as a way to reclaim such control, and then suggests that violence can be a means toward *healing* a broken relationship" ("Ezekiel," *Woman's Bible Commentary* [ed. Carol A. Newsom and Sharon H. Ringe; Louisville: Westminster John Knox, 1998], 197-98).

4. The Mountains Shall Drip Sweet Wine

1. Walter Brueggemann, "Faith at the *Nullpunkt,*" in *The End of the World and the Ends of God: Science and Theology on Eschatology* (ed. John Polkinghorne and Michael Welker; Harrisburg, Pa.: Trinity, 2000), 140, 146-47.

2. Donald E. Gowan, *Eschatology in the Old Testament* (Minneapolis: Fortress, 1986), 2.

3. Izak Cornelius, "Paradise Motifs in the 'Eschatology' of the Minor Prophets and the Iconography of the Ancient Near East: The Concepts of Fertility, Water, Trees and 'Tierfrieden' and Gen 2-3," *JNSL* 14 (1988): 42-43. Actually, the term *paradise* occurs only once in the minor prophets, namely Joel 2:3, and not in an eschatological context where the paradise is held up to contrast the destruction of the land by the locusts.

4. Cornelius, "Paradise Motifs," 54.

5. Graham S. Ogden and Richard R. Deutsch, *A Promise of Hope—A Call to Obedience: A Commentary on the Books of Joel and Malachi* (ITC; Grand Rapids, Mich.: Eerdmans, 1987), 38, 45; Bruce C. Birch, *Hosea, Joel, and Amos* (Westminster Bible Companion; Louisville: Westminster John Knox, 1997), 157-59.

6. Birch, *Hosea, Joel, and Amos* 157, 160; Dan G. Johnson, *From Chaos to Restoration: An Integrative Reading of Isaiah 24-27* (JSOTSup 61; Sheffield: Sheffield Academic Press, 1988), 53-62.

7. Ezekiel 47 is of course a foundational text for the New Testament depiction of the "river of the water of life" in Rev 22:1-2. Revelation 22 develops this image further, saying that the tree of life that grows on the riverbanks will be a source of life and vitality by bringing healing to all the nations. Ronald E. Clements, *Ezekiel* (Westminster Bible Companion; Louisville: Westminster John Knox, 1996), 204-5; Daniel I. Block, *The Book of Ezekiel* (NICOT; 2 vols.; Grand Rapids, Mich.: Eerdmans, 1997), 2:699.

8. One has to note that Ezekiel seems to deliberately disassociate God's abode from Jerusalem. The city that is described in Ezek 48:30-35 is not even located on a mountain and is not called Jerusalem but is renamed as "YHWH is there" (Steven S. Tuell, "Divine Presence and Absence in Ezekiel's Prophecy," in *The Book of Ezekiel: Theological and Anthropological Perspectives* [ed. Margaret S. Odell and John T. Strong; Atlanta: SBL, 2000], 103-4). Julie Galambush has done some interesting work regarding this disassociation of the newly restored city with Zion. She argues that a possible reason why Ezekiel avoided using female imagery relates to the fear of impurity defiling the newly restored city. After the destruction of Jerusalem, Ezekiel imagines a new city that is intentionally disassociated from Jerusalem, which exhibited clear female associations ("Jerusalem in the Book of Ezekiel: The City as Yahweh's Wife" [PhD diss., Candler School of Theology, Emory University, 1991], 259, 264, 286).

9. Patrick D. Miller, "Judgment and Joy," in *The End of the World and the Ends of God: Science and Theology on Eschatology* (ed. John Polkinghorne and Michael Welker; Harrisburg, Pa.: Trinity, 2000), 155. The dating of this text is nowhere clear, ranging, according to Miller, anywhere from the second to the eighth century. But rather than seeing this as a problem, Miller notes that the spatial and temporal flexibility of the horizon of this text provides an effective means of expressing God's consummating work.

10. Johnson, *From Chaos to Restoration*, 61; Hans Wildberger, *Isaiah 13-27: A Continental Commentary* (trans. Thomas H. Trapp; Minneapolis: Fortress, 1997), 526-31. Wildberger identifies several ancient Near Eastern texts regarding a sacrificial meal that follows upon the victory over chaos and the subsequent enthronement of the gods Baal and Marduk.

11. Miller, "Judgment and Joy," 168.

12. Johnson, *From Chaos to Restoration*, 63.

13. Brevard Childs, *Isaiah* (Louisville: Westminster John Knox, 2001), 183; Joseph Blenkinsopp, *Isaiah 1-39* (AB 19; New York: Doubleday, 2000), 359. Compare the anti-Moabite sentiment expressed in Deut 23:4-9 [3-8 MT], where the Moabites are excluded forever from the covenant community.

14. Katharine Doob Sakenfeld, *Ruth* (IBC; Louisville: John Knox, 1999), 9-11.

15. Wildberger, *Isaiah 13-27*, 533. See also the Ugaritic literature where Mot, the ruler of the underworld, swallowed Baal, thus threatening the life of the ruling deity and his purposes of creation. Johnson, *From Chaos to Restoration*, 65; Blenkinsopp, *Isaiah 1-39*, 359.

16. Wildberger, *Isaiah 13-27*, 533, 535; Miller, "Judgment and Joy," 166. Wildberger notes that Judaism after this continued to reflect on the idea that the rule of God at the end of time would also include the victory over death, that the joyous festival would only be complete when the last enemy, death, was destroyed.

17. Richard I. Pervo, "Panta Koina: The Feeding Stories in the Light of Economic Data and Social Practice," in *Religious Propoganda and Missionary Competition in the New Testament World: Essays Honoring Dieter Georgi* (ed. Lukas Bormann et al.; Leiden: E. J. Brill, 1994), 180. J. Priest makes a helpful distinction between the terms *messianic* and *eschatological* banquet. He notes that if no reference is made to the Messiah, the term *eschatological banquet* is more appropriate ("A Note on the Messianic Banquet," in *The Messiah: Developments in Earliest Judaism and Christianity* [ed. James H. Charlesworth; Minneapolis: Fortress, 1992], 222).

18. *2 Baruch 29:6-7 (OTP)*. Christian writers developed similar interpretations. For instance, the church father Irenaeus quotes Papias telling a similar story to *2 Bar 29*, where abundance is depicted even in more grandiose terms. However, in this version, the provision of food is attributed to Jesus. Gowan, *Eschatology*, 105.

19. Israel W. Slotki, trans., *Kethuboth* (vol. 2 of the *Seder Nashim*; The Babylonian Talmud; ed. I. Epstein; London: Soncino Press, 1978), *b. Ketub. 111b*.

20. *Sifre Deut.* 316 (Basser); Joseph Klausner, *The Messianic Idea in Israel from its Beginning to the Completion of the Mishnah* (London: George Allen and Unwin, 1956), 507-8; Gowan, *Eschatology*, 106.

21. *2 Baruch 29:8 (OTP)*.

22. *2 Baruch 29:5 (OTP)*. See also Gowan, *Eschatology*, 105; Pervo, "Panta Koina," 180; Priest, "Messianic Banquet," 224.

23. Dennis E. Smith, *From Symposium to Eucharist: The Banquet in the Early Christian World* (Minneapolis: Fortress, 2003), 261; Priest, "Messianic Banquet," 229-30. See also Luke 22:28-30 (and the parallel Gospel passages) and Rev 19:9 where Jesus is referred to as the host of this banquet.

24. Kenneth E. Bailey, *Through Peasant Eyes: More Lucan Parables, Their Culture and Style* (Grand Rapids, Mich.: Eerdmans, 1980), 90-91; Johnson, *From Chaos to Restoration*, 62. One has to keep in mind that "Isaiah's open-ended vision" is not as wholeheartedly inclusive as Bailey here wants to presume. Compare the discussion regarding the exclusion of the Moabites earlier in this chapter. This ambiguity is a good example of the tensions that existed in early Jewish thought.

25. Bailey, *Through Peasant Eyes*, 111.

26. Luke T. Johnson, *The Gospel of Luke* (Collegeville, Minn.: Liturgical Press, 1991), 232; Bailey, *Through Peasant Eyes*, 111.

27. Walter Harrelson, "Famine in the Perspective of Biblical Judgments and Promises," in *Lifeboat Ethics: The Moral Dilemmas of World Hunger* (ed. George R. Lucas and Thomas W. Ogletree; New York: Harper & Row, 1976), 89; Miller, "Judgment and Joy," 169.

28. Gowan, *Eschatology*, 126; Ted Peters, "The Messianic Banquet and World Hunger," *Relig. Life* 47 (1978): 506.

29. Carol J. Dempsey, "Hope Amidst Crisis: A Prophetic Vision of Cosmic Redemption," in *All Creation Is Groaning: An Interdisciplinary Vision for Life in a Sacred Universe* (ed. Carol J. Dempsey and Russell A. Butkus; Collegeville, Minn.: Liturgical Press, 1999), 280; Gowan, *Eschatology*, 120; Harrelson, "Famine," 89; Peters, "The Messianic Banquet," 506.

30. Gowan, *Eschatology*, 125.

31. Johanna W. H. van Wijk-Bos, *Reimagining God: The Case for Scriptural Diversity* (Louisville: Westminster John Knox, 1995), 63; Susan Ackerman, "Isaiah," in *Women's Bible Commentary* (ed. Carol A. Newsom and Sharon H. Ringe; Louisville: Westminster John Knox, 1998), 176. For attempts to explain why these remarkable female images were used to describe God, see Mayer I. Gruber, "The Motherhood of God in Second Isaiah," *RB* 90 (1983): 351-59; John Schmitt, "The Motherhood of God and Zion as Mother," *RB* 92 (1985): 557-69.

32. Phyllis Trible, *God and the Rhetoric of Sexuality* (OBT; Philadelphia: Fortress, 1978), 66-67. See also Trible's work regarding the links between the verb "to have compassion" (רחם) and the Hebrew root for "womb" (רחם) (pp. 33-34).

5. "*Come, Eat of My Bread and Drink of the Wine I Have Mixed*"

1. Claus Westermann, *Elements of Old Testament Theology* (Atlanta: John Knox, 1982), 11; Gerhard Hasel, *Old Testament Theology: Basic Issues in the Current Debate* (Grand Rapids, Mich.: Eerdmans, 1996), 45-46. See also Gerhard von Rad's *Old Testament Theology*, which considers Wisdom in a section called Israel's answer to God (1:355-459). Von Rad seemed dissatisfied with this treatment, and he revisited Wisdom in his *Wisdom of Israel* (Nashville: Abingdon, 1972), which typically is deemed to be the third volume of his *Old Testament Theology*.

2. This is of course a reference to Samuel Terrien's marvelous treatment of the wisdom material, *The Elusive Presence: Toward a New Biblical Theology* (San Francisco: Harper & Row, 1978), 350-80.

3. There are various suggestions why Wisdom is personified as a woman. The Hebrew word for wisdom (חכמה) as well as the Greek word (σοφία) are both female in gender. Martin Scott has suggested that the female personification developed in order to provide a means of countering the popular goddess movements by incorporating the feminine in the divine without compromising monotheism (*Sophia and the Johannine Jesus* [JSNTSup 71; Sheffield: Sheffield Academic Press, 1992], 77, 80). Two in-depth treatments of the female personification of Wisdom are the works by Claudia Camp, *Wisdom and the Feminine in the Book of Proverbs* (Sheffield: JSOT Press, 1985) and Christine Roy Yoder, *Wisdom as a Woman of Substance: A Socioeconomic Reading of Proverbs 1-9 and 31:10-31* (Berlin: Walter de Gruyter, 2001). Camp argues that the female personification of Wisdom receives its connotations from the literary representations of women throughout the Old Testament texts. Yoder suggests that this female personification draws on the lives of real women during the Persian period.

4. Karl-Gustav Sandelin, *Wisdom as Nourisher: A Study of an Old Testament Theme, Its Development within Early Judaism, and Its Impact on Early Christianity* (Åbo: Åbo Akademi, 1986); Judith E. McKinlay, *Gendering Wisdom the Host: Biblical Invitations to Eat and Drink* (JSOTSup 216; Sheffield: Sheffield Academic Press, 1996).

5. To mention but two: Raymond G. Van Leeuwen, "Proverbs," in *The New Interpreter's Bible* (ed. Leander E. Keck et al.; 12 vols.; Nashville: Abingdon, 1997), 5:17-264; Michael Fox, *Proverbs 1-9* (AB 18A; New York: Doubleday, 2000).

6. McKinlay, *Gendering Wisdom the Host*, 48. In contrast to the life-giving feast of Woman Wisdom, her counterpart, Dame Folly as she typically is referred to, holds another

banquet in Prov 9:13-18. But in contrast to Woman Wisdom's banquet that leads to life, Folly's gifts of foods, no matter how sweet or pleasant to the taste (v. 17), lead to death.

7. Fox, *Proverbs 1-9*, 297-98.

8. McKinlay, *Gendering Wisdom the Host*, 55; Leo G. Perdue, *Wisdom and Creation: The Theology of Wisdom Literature* (Nashville: Abingdon, 1994), 95-96.

9. McKinlay, *Gendering Wisdom the Host*, 55-56.

10. Joachim Begrich, *Studien zu Deuterojesaja* (ed. Walther Zimmerli; Munich: Kaiser, 1963), 59-60; Claus Westermann, *Isaiah 40-66: A Commentary* (trans. David M. G. Stalker; Philadelphia: Westminster, 1969), 281. See also R. J. Clifford, "Isaiah 55: Invitation to a Feast," in *The Word of the Lord Shall Go Forth: Festschrift for D. N. Freedman* (ed. C. L. Meyers and M. O'Connor; Winona Lake, Ind.: Eisenbrauns, 1983), 28-30. Clifford offers parallel texts describing a Ugaritic royal banquet scene as an interpretative framework for the invitation to the feast in Isa 55 and Prov 9.

11. Gene Rice, "Dining with Deutero-Isaiah," *JRT* 37 (1980): 23.

12. McKinlay, *Gendering Wisdom the Host*, 133.

13. J. Israelstam, trans., *Leviticus* (vol. 4 of *Midrash Rabbah*; ed. H. Freeman and Maurice Simon; London: Soncino Press, 1939), 11:1.

14. Van Leeuwen, "Proverbs," 100-102. Van Leeuwen argues that in the ancient Near East, cultic houses were considered to function as "microcosmic reflections of the macrocosmic world of God's creation" (e.g., Ps 78:69).

15. Scott, *Sophia and the Johannine Jesus*, 51; Roland E. Murphy, *Proverbs* (WBC; Dallas: Word, 1998), 52. Compare the controversy concerning the interpretation of Wisdom's origins. In Prov 8:22, Wisdom is said to have existed before anything else in the world, either being "created" or "acquired" by God, depending on how one interprets the word קָנָנִי. Scholars are divided on how to interpret this text—something mirrored in the division among the earliest versions. Whether one interprets Wisdom as being "acquired" or "begotten" by God depends much on what picture one has of Woman Wisdom (Perdue, *Wisdom and Creation*, 355).

16. This controversy derives from the uncertainty concerning the interpretation of אָמוֹן, which could either be taken as a noun, "craftsperson" (*'āmōn*), or a Qal passive participle, "favorite child" (*'āmûn*). Karen Jobes points out that most English translations support the former interpretation. The LXX chose neither of these interpretations and, rather, interprets the Hebrew by using the Greek participle ἁρμόζουσα, meaning "to be in harmony with." The Greek interpreters Aquila, Symmachus, and Theodotian chose the translation of "God's child," which gives her not an active role in creation but that of a witness. Johan Cook argues that the Greek translations want to eliminate any possible ambiguity that would suggest that Wisdom is in any way responsible for creation. Karen H. Jobes, "Sophia Christology: The Way of Wisdom," in *The Way of Wisdom: Essays in Honor of Bruce K. Waltke* (ed. J. I. Packer and Sven K. Soderlund; Grand Rapids, Mich.: Zondervan, 2000), 230-31; Johan Cook, *The Septuagint of Proverbs: Jewish and/or Hellenistic Proverbs?* (Leiden: E. J. Brill, 1997), 224, 292.

17. H. Freedman, trans., *Genesis* (vol. 1 of *Midrash Rabbah*; ed. H. Freedman and Maurice Simon; London: Soncino Press, 1983), 1:1; Van Leeuwen, "Proverbs," 102.

18. Van Leeuwen, "Proverbs," 103-4.

19. Terrien, *Elusive Presence*, 360. Gale Yee has identified the erotic imagery that surrounds Woman Wisdom and the foreign woman in Prov 1–9. In light of these connections, she points out the unsettling message at the heart of this text, namely that the text

seems to propagate that "only man pursues Wisdom like a lover, and it is a woman who seduces him away from her" ("'I Have Perfumed My Bed with Myrrh': The Foreign Woman '*issa zara* in Proverbs 1-9," *JSOT* 43 [1989]: 53-68). See also McKinlay, *Gendering Wisdom the Host*, 63.

20. Ibid., *Wisdom as Nourisher*, 38.

21. Ibid., 33.

22. Peder Borgen, *Philo of Alexandria: An Exegete for His Time* (Leiden: E. J. Brill, 1997), 47. This is mainly due to the exegetical method Philo employs, which Borgen identifies as containing several midrashic features. Compare Peder Borgen, *Bread from Heaven: An Exegetical Study of the Concept of Manna in the Gospel of John and the Writings of Philo* (Leiden: E. J. Brill, 1965), 1-59.

23. Philo typically allegorizes the manna. See also *Leg.* 3:162-81 where manna is interpreted as the heavenly bread of the word of God and as the food of light, which should be taken daily. Borgen, *Bread from Heaven*, 14, 99-146.

24. Philo, *Det.* 115–118 (Colson and Whitaker, LCL).

25. This interpretation reminds one of the midrash in *Exod. Rab.* 1:12 and *b. Soṭah 11b* (ch. 1) that narrates the story of God providing two balls or cakes for the children of Israel to suckle on—the one with oil and the one with honey. The prooftext in this midrash is also Deut 32:13—the same one Philo uses. This is a classic example of the similarities that exist between Philo and midrash. The debate concerning the relationship between Philo and the midrashic tradition is, however, beyond the scope of this study.

26. One should keep in mind that the christological development is highly complex with many other influences besides the Wisdom influences contributing to its final form.

27. Elizabeth A. Johnson, "Jesus, the Wisdom of God: A Biblical Basis for Non-Androcentric Christology," *ETL* 61 (1985): 261. Compare Brown's representative statement: "In John, Jesus is personified Wisdom" (Raymond Brown, *The Gospel according to John* [AB 29; 2 vols.; New York: Doubleday, 1966], 1:cxxiv); James Dunn, "Was Christianity a Monotheistic Faith from the Beginning?" *SJT* 35 (1982): 330.

28. Murphy, *Proverbs*, 281.

29. Johnson, "Jesus, The Wisdom of God," 273.

30. Ibid., 273-74; Dunn, "Christianity," 318-21.

31. Terrien, *Elusive Presence*, 360.

32. Roland E. Murphy, "The Personification of Wisdom," in *Wisdom in Ancient Israel: Essays in Honour of J. S. Emerton* (ed. John Day, et al.; Cambridge: Cambridge University Press, 1995), 222-33.

33. Johnson, "Jesus, The Wisdom of God," 275. Compare Scott's conclusion: "Just as Yahweh is an expression of the one God (*male*), so too Sophia is an expression of the one God (*female*)" (*Sophia and the Johannine Jesus*, 77).

34. McKinlay, *Gendering Wisdom the Host*, 247. Compare the many feminist theologians who have decided that this reality makes Yahweh and the Christian/Jewish religions irredeemable. For example, Daphne Hampson argues for a total reshaping of the traditional male God. Such a reshaping includes the reclaiming of goddess traditions (*Theology and Feminism* [Oxford: Basil Blackwell, 1990], 148-75).

35. McKinlay, *Gendering Wisdom the Host*, 143-59.

36. Scott, *Sophia and the Johannine Jesus*, 79; Johnson, "Jesus, The Wisdom of God," 287.

37. McKinlay, *Gendering Wisdom the Host*, 133.

38. Ibid., 244.

6. God's Provision of Food in the New Testament and Beyond

1. Joel B. Green, *The Gospel of Luke* (NICNT; Grand Rapids, Mich.: Eerdmans, 1997), 363. See also the links with the stories told in 1 Kgs 17:8-16 and 2 Kgs 4:42-44, where, respectively, Elijah and Elisha are said to provide food by means of the God who feeds. Joseph A. Fitzmyer, *The Gospel according to Luke I-IX: Introduction, Translation, Notes* (AB 28; New York: Doubleday, 1981), 766.

2. Green, *Luke*, 365.

3. Compare the comprehensive work by Jane S. Webster, *Ingesting Jesus: Eating and Drinking in the Gospel of John* (Academia Biblica 6; Atlanta: Society of Biblical Literature, 2003).

4. Peder Borgen, *Bread from Heaven: An Exegetical Study of the Concept of Manna in the Gospel of John and the Writings of Philo* (Leiden: E. J. Brill, 1965), 61-64; Raymond Brown, *The Gospel according to John* (AB 29; 2 vols.; New York: Doubleday, 1966), 1:262; Bruce G. Schuchard, *Scripture within Scripture: The Interrelationship of Form and Function in the Explicit Old Testament Citations in the Gospel of John* (SBLDS 133; Atlanta: Scholars Press, 1992), 39, 45-46.

5. Schuchard, *Scripture within Scripture*, 40, 44; Dennis E. Smith, *From Symposium to Eucharist: The Banquet in the Early Christian World* (Minneapolis: Fortress, 2003), 274. Smith notes that although John does not have the traditional Last Supper scene, Jesus' words over the bread and wine in John 6:53-54 suggest some eucharistic undertones. See also Borgen, *Bread from Heaven*, 186; Brown, *John*, 1:274-75; Karl-Gustav Sandelin, *Wisdom as Nourisher: A Study of an Old Testament Theme, Its Development within Early Judaism, and Its Impact on Early Christianity* (Åbo: Åbo Akademi, 1986), 174.

6. Elizabeth A. Johnson, "Jesus, The Wisdom of God: A Biblical Basis for Non-Androcentric Christology," *ETL* 61 (1985): 280.

7. Ibid., 294.

8. Judith E. McKinlay, *Gendering Wisdom the Host: Biblical Invitations to Eat and Drink* (JSOTSup 216; Sheffield: Sheffield Academic Press, 1996), 239-40.

9. Ibid., 252.

10. David F. Ford, *Self and Salvation: Being Transformed* (Cambridge Studies in Christian Doctrine; Cambridge: Cambridge University Press, 1999), 163. See also the description in ch. 1 of the "ritualization of metaphors," which David Marcus identifies regarding medieval Jewish rituals.

11. "Baptism, Eucharist, Ministry" (Faith and Order Paper 111; Geneva: World Council of Churches, 1982). For a good overview about the current issues in the discussion on the sacrament of the Eucharist, cf. Michael Welker, *What Happens in Holy Communion?* (trans. John F. Hoffmeyer; Grand Rapids, Mich.: Eerdmans, 2000).

12. Ford, *Self and Salvation*, 154.

13. Jan Assmann, *Das kulturelle Gedächtnis: Schrift, Erinnerung und politische Identität in frühen Hochkulturen* (Munich: Beck, 1992); Welker, *Holy Communion*, 127-29.

14. Luke T. Johnson, "Imagining the World Scripture Imagines," in *Theology and Scriptural Imagination* (ed. L. Gregory Jones and James J. Buckley; Oxford: Blackwell, 1998), 44.

15. Welker, *Holy Communion*, 103.

16. Ford, *Self and Salvation*, 147.

17. "Baptism, Eucharist, Ministry," gives the following commentary on the matter:

> Many churches believe that by the words of Jesus and by the power of the Holy Spirit, the bread and wine of the eucharist become, in a real though mysterious manner, the body and blood of the risen Christ.... Some other churches, while affirming a real presence of Christ at the eucharist, do not link that presence so definitely with the signs of bread and wine. The decision remains for the churches whether this difference can be accommodated within the convergence formulated in the text itself. (BEM 2B13, Commentary)

See also the chapter regarding the "real presence" of Christ in the Eucharist in Michael Welker's book, *What Happens in Holy Communion?* 87-100.

18. David F. Ford, *Self and Salvation: Being Transformed* (Cambridge: Cambridge University Press, 1999), 269.

19. However, as the sad history of, for example, the Dutch Reformed Church attests, the sacrament of the Eucharist can be very divisive. It is generally known that one of the first noted instances of apartheid relates to a decision made by the church leadership of the Swellendam congregation in 1857 who decided on separate occasions of the Eucharist for "members from the heathen," as the new black converts were called. The reason that was given for this decision was because of the weakness of some (white) members of the congregation. What initially began as a temporary situation, as a concession to the weak, ultimately became "solidified, rationalized" and "formalized" into the doctrine of apartheid. Stephen E. Fowl and L. Gregory Jones, *Reading in Communion: Scripture and Ethics in Christian Life* (London: SPCK, 1991), 97; William C. Placher, *Narratives of a Vulnerable God: Christ, Theology, and Scripture* (Louisville: Westminster John Knox, 1995), 155.

20. Welker, *Holy Communion*, 175.

21. Elizabeth A. Johnson, *She Who Is: The Mystery of God in Feminist Theological Discourse* (New York: Crossroad, 1992), 176-77.

22. Johanna Kohn-Roelin, "Mother-Daughter-God," in *Motherhood: Experience, Institution, Theology* (ed. Anne Carr and Elisabeth Schüssler Fiorenza; Edinburgh: T&T Clark, 1989), 65; Ursula King, "The Divine as Mother," in *Motherhood: Experience, Institution, Theology* (ed. Anne Carr and Elisabeth Schüssler Fiorenza; Edinburgh: T&T Clark, 1989), 136; Sallie McFague "Mother God," in *The Power of Naming: A Concilium Reader in Feminist Liberation Theology* (ed. Elisabeth Schüssler Fiorenza; Maryknoll, N.Y.: Orbis Books, 1996), 325; Johnson, *She Who Is*, 178, 186. McFague argues that one should refrain from establishing a new hierarchical dualism. The danger in such a dualism is that people are kept in the role of perpetual children. To avoid this, one may argue as Johnson does that "it is human experience that we do not remain small children, but grow up into adults." Moreover, as one's relationship with one's own mother and the mothering persons in one's life matures, it may grow to incorporate elements of mutual friendship and help.

23. Rita Nakashima Brock, "The Greening of the Soul: A Feminist Theological Paradigm of the Web of Life," in *Setting the Table: Women in Theological Conversation* (ed. Rita Nakashima Brock et al.; St. Louis: Chalice, 1995), 151; Johnson, *She Who Is*, 178.

24. Compare, e.g., the Roman Catholic document *Inter Insigniores* that holds the following position on the maleness of the priest:

> The same natural resemblance is required for persons as for things: when Christ's role in the Eucharist is to be expressed sacramentally, there would not be this "natural resemblance" which must exist between Christ and his minister if the role of Christ were not taken by a man: in such a case it would be difficult to see in the minister the image of Christ. For Christ himself was and remains a man. (*Inter Insigniores* 27)

For a good overview of the various ways in which feminist theologians have dealt with this issue, see Elisabeth Schüssler Fiorenza, *Jesus, Miriam's Child, Sophia's Prophet: Critical Issues in Feminist Christology* (New York: Continuum, 1994), 43-49.

25. Quoted in McKinlay, *Gendering Wisdom the Host*, 248. From "Another Fragment," (ANF 5:175).

26. McKinlay, *Gendering Wisdom the Host*, 249.

SELECTED BIBLIOGRAPHY

Translations

Basser, Herbert W., ed. *Midrashic Interpretations of the Song of Moses*. New York: P. Lang, 1984.

Braude, William, and Israel J. Kapstein, eds. *Pesiqta de Rab Kahana: R. Kahana's Compilation of Discourses for Sabbaths and Festal Days*. Philadelphia: Jewish Publication Society of America, 1975.

Charlesworth, James H., ed. *The Old Testament Pseudepigrapha*. 2 vols. New York: Doubleday, 1985.

Colson, F. H., and G. H. Whitaker, eds. *Philo: With an English Translation*. 10 vols. and 2 supplementary vols. Loeb Classical Library. Cambridge, Mass.: Harvard University Press, 1929. Repr., 1991.

Epstein, I., ed. *The Babylonian Talmud*. 18 vols. Quincentenary edition. London: Soncino, 1978.

———. *Yoma, Sukkah, Bezah*. Translated by Leo Jung. Vol. 4 of *The Babylonian Talmud*. 18 vols. Quincentenary edition. London: Soncino, 1978.

Freedman, H., and Maurice Simon, eds. *Midrash Rabbah*. 10 vols. London: Soncino, 1939. Repr., 1983.

———. *Exodus*. Translated by S. M. Lehrman. Vol. 3 of *Midrash Rabbah*. London: Soncino, 1983.

———. *Lamentations*. Translated by A. Cohen. Vol. 7 of *Midrash Rabbah*. London: Soncino, 1983.

———. *Leviticus*. Translated by J. Israelstam. Vol. 4 of *Midrash Rabbah*. London: Soncino, 1983.

———. *The Song of Songs*. Translated by Maurice Simon. Vol. 9 of *Midrash Rabbah*. London: Soncino, 1983.

Jerusalmi, Isaac, ed. *Song of Songs in the Targumic Tradition: Vocalized Aramaic Text with Facing English Translation and Ladino Versions. Aramaic Concordance, Aramaic-English, Ladino-English Glossaries*. Cincinnati: Ladino Books, 1993.

Lauterbach, Jacob Z., ed. *Mekilta de-Rabbi Ishmael: A Critical Edition on the Basis of the Manuscripts and Early Editions with an English Translation, Introduction and Notes*. 3 vols. Philadelphia: Jewish Publication Society of America, 1933.

Nemoy, Leon, ed. *The Midrash on Psalms*. Translated by William G. Braude. Yale Judaica Series 13. New Haven: Yale University Press, 1959.

Neusner, Jacob, ed. *Sifre to Numbers: An American Translation and Explanation*. 2 vols. Atlanta: Sanders, 1986.

On Metaphor and Biblical Interpretation

Avis, Paul. *God and the Creative Imagination: Metaphor, Symbol and Myth in Religion and Theology.* London: Routledge, 1999.

Brettler, Marc Z. "The Metaphorical Mapping of God in the Hebrew Bible." Pages 219-32 in *Metaphor, Canon and Community: Jewish, Christian and Islamic approaches.* Edited by Ralph Bisschops and James Francis. Bern: Peter Lang, 1999.

Brown, William P. "The Metaphorical Imagination and Biblical Interpretation." Pages 1-25 in *God and the Imagination: A Primer to Reading the Psalms in an Age of Pluralism.* The 2000 J. J. Thiessen Lectures. Winnipeg, MB: CMBC Publications, 2001.

———. *Seeing the Psalms: A Theology of Metaphor.* Louisville: Westminster John Knox, 2002.

Johnson, Luke T. "Imagining the World Scripture Imagines." Pages 3-18 in *Theology and Scriptural Imagination.* Edited by L. Gregory Jones and James J. Buckley. Oxford: Blackwell, 1998.

Soskice, Janet Martin. *Metaphor and Religious Language.* Oxford: Clarendon, 1985.

On Feminist Biblical Interpretation

Bach, Alice, ed. *Women in the Hebrew Bible: A Reader.* New York: Routledge, 1999.

Brock, Rita Nakashima, Claudia Camp, and Serene Jones, eds. *Setting the Table: Women in Theological Conversation.* St. Louis: Chalice, 1995.

Carr, Anne, and Elisabeth Schüssler Fiorenza, eds. *Motherhood: Experience, Institution, Theology.* Edinburgh: T&T Clark, 1989.

Johnson, Elizabeth A. "Jesus, the Wisdom of God: A Biblical Basis for Non-Androcentric Christology." *Ephemerides Theologicae Lovanienses* 61 (1985): 261-94.

———. *She Who Is: The Mystery of God in Feminist Theological Discourse.* New York: Crossroad, 1992.

McFague, Sallie. *Models of God: Theology for an Ecological Nuclear Age.* Philadelphia: Fortress, 1987.

———. "Mother God." Pages 324-29 in *The Power of Naming: A Concilium Reader in Feminist Liberation Theology.* Edited by Elisabeth Schüssler Fiorenza. Maryknoll, N.Y.: Orbis Books, 1996.

Meyers, Carol. *Discovering Eve: Ancient Israelite Women in Context.* New York: Oxford University Press, 1988.

———. "Women and the Domestic Economy of Early Israel." Pages 265-81 in *Women's Earliest Records from Ancient Egypt and Western Asia.* Edited by Barbara Lesko. Atlanta: Scholars Press, 1989.

Newsom, Carol A., and Sharon H. Ringe, eds. *Women's Bible Commentary.* Louisville: Westminster John Knox, 1998.

Schüssler Fiorenza, Elisabeth. *But She Said: Feminist Practices of Biblical Interpretation.* Boston: Beacon, 1992.

Trible, Phyllis. *God and the Rhetoric of Sexuality.* Overtures to Biblical Theology. Philadelphia: Fortress, 1978.

van Wijk-Bos, Johanna W. H. *Reimagining God: The Case for Scriptural Diversity.* Louisville: Westminster John Knox, 1995.

On Midrash

Bloch, Renée. "Midrash." Pages 29-50 in vol. 1 of *Approaches to Ancient Judaism: Theory and Practice*. Edited by William Scott Green. Translated by Mary Howard Callaway. Brown Judaic Studies. 5 vols. Missoula, Mont.: Scholars Press for Brown University, 1978.
Porton, Gary. "Defining Midrash." Pages 55-92 in *The Study of Ancient Judaism*. Edited by Jacob Neusner. New York: Ktav, 1981.
Wright, Addison G. *The Literary Genre Midrash*. New York: Alba House, 1967.

On Bakhtin and Biblical Theology

Claassens, L. Juliana M. "Biblical Theology as Dialogue: Continuing the Conversation on Bakhtin and Biblical Theology." *Journal of Biblical Literature* 122 (2003): 127-45.
Newsom, Carol A. "Bakhtin, the Bible and Dialogic Truth." *Journal of Religion* 76 (1996): 290-306.
Olson, Dennis T. "Biblical Theology as Provisional Monologization: A Dialogue with Childs, Brueggemann and Bakhtin." *Biblical Interpretation* 6 (1998): 162-80.

Other Selected Works

Andersen, Francis I., and David Noel Freedman. *Amos: A New Translation with Introduction and Commentary*. Anchor Bible 24A. New York: Doubleday, 1989.
Anderson, Bernard W. *From Creation to New Creation*. Old Testament Perspectives. Minneapolis: Fortress, 1994.
Bailey, Kenneth E. "The Great Banquet." Pages 88-113 in *Through Peasant Eyes: More Lukan Parables*. Grand Rapids, Mich.: Eerdmans, 1980.
Beuken, Wim, Marieke Den Hartog, Jaap van der Meij, Marcel Poorthuis, Ben Vedder, and Wim Weren, eds. *Brood uit de Hemel: Lijnen van Exodus 16 naar Johannes 6 tegen de Achtergrond van de Rabbijnse Literatuur*. Kampen: J. H. Kok, 1985.
Billman, Kathleen D., and Daniel L. Migliore. *Rachel's Cry: Prayer of Lament and Rebirth of Hope*. Cleveland: United Church Press, 1999.
Birch, Bruce C. *Hosea, Joel, and Amos*. Westminster Bible Companion. Louisville: Westminster John Knox, 1997.
Block, Daniel I. *The Book of Ezekiel*. The New International Commentary on the Old Testament. 2 vols. Grand Rapids, Mich.: Eerdmans, 1997.
Blumenthal, David R. *Facing the Abusing God: A Theology of Protest*. Louisville: Westminster/John Knox, 1993.
Borgen, Peder. *Bread From Heaven: An Exegetical Study of the Concept of Manna in the Gospel of John and the Writings of Philo*. Leiden: E. J. Brill, 1965.
Brenner, Athalya, and Jan Willem van Henten, eds. *Food and Drink in the Biblical Worlds*. Semeia 86. Atlanta: Society of Biblical Literature, 1999.
Brueggemann, Walter. "Faith at the *Nullpunkt*." Pages 143-54 in *The End of the World and the Ends of God: Science and Theology on Eschatology*. Edited by John Polkinghorne and Michael Welker. Harrisburg, Pa.: Trinity, 2000.
———. *Message of the Psalms*. Augsburg Old Testament Studies. Minneapolis: Augsburg, 1984.

―――. "A Subversive Memory in a Sacramental Container." *Reformed Liturgy and Music* 19 (1985): 34-38.

―――. *Theology of the Old Testament: Testimony, Dispute, Advocacy*. Minneapolis: Fortress, 1997.

Camp, Claudia V. *Wisdom and the Feminine in the Book of Proverbs*. Sheffield: JSOT Press, 1985.

Claassens, L. Juliana M. "The God Who Feeds: A Feminist-Theological Analysis of Key Pentateuchal and Intertestamental Texts." PhD diss., Princeton Theological Seminary, 2001.

Cornelius, Izak. "Paradise Motifs in the 'Eschatology' of the Minor Prophets and the Iconography of the Ancient Near East: The Concepts of Fertility, Water, Trees and 'Tierfrieden' and Gen 2-3." *Journal of Northwest Semitic Languages* 14 (1988): 41-83.

Demsey, Carol J., and Russell A. Butkus, eds. *All Creation Is Groaning: An Interdisciplinary Vision for Life in a Sacred Universe*. Collegeville, Minn.: Liturgical Press, 2001.

Dobbs-Allsopp, F. W. *Lamentations*. Interpretation: A Bible Commentary for Teaching and Preaching. Louisville: John Knox, 2002.

Farley, Wendy. *Tragic Vision and Divine Compassion: A Contemporary Theodicy*. Louisville: Westminster/John Knox, 1990.

Fitzmyer, Joseph A. *The Gospel according to Luke I-IX: Introduction, Translation, Notes*. Anchor Bible 28. New York: Doubleday, 1981.

―――. *The Gospel according to Luke X-XXIV: Introduction, Translation, Notes*. Anchor Bible 28A. New York: Doubleday, 1985.

Ford, David F. *Self and Salvation: Being Transformed*. Cambridge Studies in Christian Doctrine. Cambridge: Cambridge University Press, 1999.

Fox, Michael. *Proverbs 1-9*. Anchor Bible 18A. New York: Doubleday, 2000.

Gowan, Donald E. *Eschatology in the Old Testament*. Minneapolis: Fortress, 1986.

Green, Joel B. *The Gospel of Luke*. New International Commentary on the New Testament. Grand Rapids, Mich.: Eerdmans, 1997.

Habel, Norman C. *The Book of Job*. Philadelphia: Westminster, 1985.

Harrelson, Walter. "Famine in the Perspective of Biblical Judgments and Promises." Pages 84-99 in *Lifeboat Ethics: The Moral Dilemmas of World Hunger*. Edited by George R. Lucas and Thomas W. Ogletree. New York: Harper & Row, 1976.

Houtman, Cornelis. *Exodus*. Translated by Sierd Woudstra and Johan Rebel. Historical Commentary on the Old Testament. Leuven: Peeters, 1993. Repr., Kampen: J. H. Kok, 1996.

Johnson, Luke T. *The Gospel of Luke*. Collegeville, Minn.: Liturgical Press, 1991.

Knierim, Rolf P. *The Task of Old Testament Theology: Substance, Method, and Cases*. Grand Rapids, Mich.: Eerdmans, 1995.

Kolitz, Zvi. *Yosl Rakover Talks to God*. Translated by Carol Brown Janeway. New York: Pantheon Books, 1999.

Kratz, Reinhard Gregor. "Die Gnade des täglichen Brots: Späte Psalmen auf dem Weg zum Vaterunser." *Zeitschrift für Theologie und Kirche* 89 (1992): 1-40.

Kraus, Hans-Joachim. *Psalms 60-150: A Commentary*. Translated by Hilton C. Oswald. Minneapolis: Augsburg, 1989.

Linafelt, Tod. *Surviving Lamentations: Catastrophe, Lament and Protest in the Afterlife of a Biblical Book*. Chicago: University of Chicago Press, 2000.

Marcus, Ivan G. *Rituals of Childhood: Jewish Acculturation in Medieval Europe*. New Haven: Yale University Press, 1996.

Mays, James L. *Amos: A Commentary*. Old Testament Library. Philadelphia: Westminster, 1969.

———. "'Maker of Heaven and Earth': Creation in the Psalms." Pages 75-86 in *God Who Creates: Essays in Honor of W. Sibley Towner*. Edited by William P. Brown and S. Dean McBride Jr. Grand Rapids, Mich.: Eerdmans, 2000.

McFague, Sallie. *Life Abundant: Rethinking Theology and Economy for a Planet in Peril*. Minneapolis: Fortress, 2001.

McKinlay, Judith E. *Gendering Wisdom the Host: Biblical Invitations to Eat and Drink*. Journal for the Study of the Old Testament: Supplement Series 216. Sheffield: Sheffield Academic Press, 1996.

Miller, Patrick D. *Deuteronomy*. Interpretation: A Bible Commentary for Teaching and Preaching. Louisville: Westminster John Knox, 1990.

———. "Judgment and Joy." Pages 155-70 in *The End of the World and the Ends of God: Science and Theology on Eschatology*. Edited by John Polkinghorne and Michael Welker. Harrisburg, Pa.: Trinity, 2000.

———. "The Poetry of Creation: Psalm 104." Pages 87-103 in *God Who Creates: Essays in Honor of W. Sibley Towner*. Edited by William P. Brown and S. Dean McBride Jr. Grand Rapids, Mich.: Eerdmans, 2000.

———. *They Cried to the Lord: The Form and Theology of Biblical Prayer*. Minneapolis: Fortress, 1994.

Murphy, Roland E. *Proverbs*. Word Biblical Commentary. Dallas: Word, 1998.

Newsom, Carol A. "The Moral Sense of Nature: Ethics in the Light of God's Speech to Job." *Princeton Seminary Bulletin* 15 (1994): 9-27.

O'Connor, Kathleen. "The Book of Lamentations: Introduction, Commentary, Reflection." Pages 1011-72 in *The New Interpreter's Bible*. Edited by Leander E. Keck et al. 12 vols. Nashville: Abingdon, 2001.

Ogden, Graham S. and Richard R. Deutsch. *A Promise of Hope—A Call to Obedience: A Commentary on the Books of Joel and Malachi*. International Theological Commentary. Grand Rapids, Mich.: Eerdmans, 1987.

Olson, Dennis T. *The Death of the Old and the Birth of the New: The Framework of the Book of Numbers and the Pentateuch*. Chico, Calif.: Scholars Press, 1985.

———. *Deuteronomy and the Death of Moses: A Theological Reading*. Minneapolis: Fortress, 1994.

———. *Numbers*. Interpretation: A Bible Commentary for Teaching and Preaching. Louisville: Westminster John Knox, 1996.

Perdue, Leo G. *Wisdom and Creation: The Theology of Wisdom Literature*. Nashville: Abingdon, 1994.

Peters, Ted. "The Messianic Banquet and World Hunger." *Religion in Life* 47 (1978): 497-508.

Priest, J. "A Note on the Messianic Banquet." Pages 222-38 in *The Messiah: Developments in Earliest Judaism and Christianity*. Edited by James H. Charlesworth. Minneapolis: Fortress, 1992.

Propp, William H. C. *Exodus 1-18: A New Translation with Introduction and Commentary*. Anchor Bible 2. New York: Doubleday, 1999.

Risse, Siegfried. "'Wir Sind die Jungen Raben!' Zur Auslegunsgeschichte von Ps. 147:9b." *Biblical Interpretation* 7 (1999): 369-88.

Sakenfeld, Katharine Doob. *Ruth*. Interpretation: A Bible Commentary for Teaching and Preaching. Louisville: John Knox, 1999.

Sandelin, Karl-Gustav. *Wisdom as Nourisher: A Study of an Old Testament Theme, Its Development within Early Judaism, and Its Impact on Early Christianity.* Åbo: Åbo Akademi, 1986.

Scott, Martin. *Sophia and the Johannine Jesus.* Journal for the Study of the New Testament: Supplement Series 71. Sheffield: Sheffield Academic Press, 1992.

Smith, Dennis E. *From Symposium to Eucharist: The Banquet in the Early Christian World.* Minneapolis: Fortress, 2003.

Terrien, Samuel. *The Elusive Presence: Toward a New Biblical Theology.* San Francisco: Harper & Row, 1978.

Van Leeuwen, Raymond G. "Proverbs." Pages 17-264 in *The New Interpreter's Bible.* Edited by Leander E. Keck et al. 12 vols. Nashville: Abingdon, 1997.

Welker, Michael. *What Happens in Holy Communion?* Translated by John F. Hoffmeyer. Grand Rapids, Mich.: Eerdmans, 2000.

Westermann, Claus. *Genesis 1-11: A Commentary.* Translated by John J. Scullion. Minneapolis: Augsburg, 1984.

———. *Isaiah 40-66: A Commentary.* Translated by David M. G. Stalker. Philadelphia: Westminster, 1969.

Wildberger, Hans. *Isaiah 13-27: A Continental Commentary.* Translated by Thomas H. Trapp. Minneapolis: Fortress, 1997.

Wolff, Hans Walter. *Joel and Amos.* Translated by Waldemar Janzen et al. Hermeneia: A Critical and Historical Commentary on the Bible. Edited by S. Dean McBride Jr. Philadelphia: Fortress, 1977.

Yoder, Christine Roy. *Wisdom as a Woman of Substance: A Socioeconomic Reading of Proverbs 1-9 and 31:10-31.* Berlin: Walter de Gruyter, 2001.

Scripture Index

Old Testament

Genesis

Exodus

Leviticus

Numbers

New Testament

Targumic Texts

Targum Song of Songs
4:5 16

Targum Isaiah
25:6 77

Rabbinic Works

Midrash Tehillim
104.17 32
146.4 34
146.6 36

Pesiqta Rabbati
8 123

Pesiqta de Rab Kahana
12 16
15:4 123

Genesis Rabbah
1:1 89
43:6 117
54:1 117
70:5 117

Exodus Rabbah
1:12 . . . . 4, 129
31:10 123

Leviticus Rabbah
11:1 88-89

Numbers Rabbah
8:9 117
13:15, 16 117

Lamentations Rabbah
24 . . . . 58, 59

Canticles Rabbah
4:5 16

Ecclesiastes Rabbah
7:8 117

Sifre Deuteronomy
316 76

Sifre Numbers
89 . . . . 3, 4

Talmud

Babylonian Ketubbot
111b 75

Babylonian Soṭah
11b 4, 129

Babylonian Yoma
75a 2, 3

Clement

Paedagogus
I.6.46.1 20

Hippolytus

"Another Fragment" (*ANF* 5:175)
Proverbs 9:1 110